HOW TO
CONDUCT
INTERVIEWS
BY TELEPHONE
AND
IN PERSON

THE SURVEY KIT

Purpose: The purposes of this 9-volume Kit are to enable readers to prepare and conduct surveys and become better users of survey results. Surveys are conducted to collect information by asking questions of people on the telephone, face-to-face, and by mail. The questions can be about attitudes, beliefs, and behavior as well as socioeconomic and health status. To do a good survey also means knowing how to ask questions, design the survey (research) project, sample respondents, collect reliable and valid information, and analyze and report the results. You also need to know how to plan and budget for your survey.

Users: The Kit is for students in undergraduate and graduate classes in the social and health sciences and for individuals in the public and private sectors who are responsible for conducting and using surveys. Its primary goal is to enable users to prepare surveys and collect data that are accurate and useful for primarily practical purposes. Sometimes, these practical purposes overlap the objectives of scientific research, and so survey researchers will also find the Kit useful.

Format of the Kit: All books in the series contain instructional objectives, exercises and answers, examples of surveys in use and illustrations of survey questions, guidelines for action, checklists of do's and don'ts, and annotated references.

Volumes in The Survey Kit:

1. **The Survey Handbook**
   Arlene Fink

2. **How to Ask Survey Questions**
   Arlene Fink

3. **How to Conduct Self-Administered and Mail Surveys**
   Linda B. Bourque and *Eve P. Fielder*

4. **How to Conduct Interviews by Telephone and in Person**
   James H. Frey and *Sabine Mertens Oishi*

5. **How to Design Surveys**
   Arlene Fink

6. **How to Sample in Surveys**
   Arlene Fink

7. **How to Measure Survey Reliability and Validity**
   Mark S. Litwin

8. **How to Analyze Survey Data**
   Arlene Fink

9. **How to Report on Surveys**
   Arlene Fink

THE SURVEY KIT

TSK✓4

HOW TO CONDUCT INTERVIEWS BY TELEPHONE AND IN PERSON

JAMES H. FREY &
SABINE MERTENS OISHI

SAGE Publications
International Educational and Professional Publisher
Thousand Oaks   London   New Delhi

For information address:

SAGE Publications, Inc.
2455 Teller Road
Thousand Oaks, California 91320
E-mail: order@sagepub.com

SAGE Publications Ltd.
6 Bonhill Street
London EC2A 4PU
United Kingdom

SAGE Publications India Pvt. Ltd.
M-32 Market
Greater Kailash I
New Delhi 110 048 India

Printed in the United States of America

Library of Congress Cataloging-in-Publication Data

Main entry under title:

The survey kit.
    p. cm.
    Includes bibliographical references.
    Contents: v. 1. The survey handbook / Arlene Fink — v. 2. How to ask survey questions / Arlene Fink — v. 3. How to conduct self-administered and mail surveys / Linda B. Bourque, Eve P. Fielder — v. 4. How to conduct interviews by telephone and in person / James H. Frey, Sabine Mertens Oishi — v. 5. How to design surveys / Arlene Fink — v. 6. How to sample in surveys / Arlene Fink — v. 7. How to measure survey reliability and validity / Mark S. Litwin — v. 8. How to analyze survey data / Arlene Fink — v. 9. How to report on surveys / Arlene Fink.
    ISBN 0-8039-7388-8 (pbk. : The survey kit : alk. paper)
    1. Social surveys. 2. Health surveys. I. Fink, Arlene.
HN29.S724   1995
300'.723—dc20   95-12712

This book is printed on acid-free paper.

  96 97 98 99 10 9 8 7 6 5 4 3 2

Sage Production Editor: Diane S. Foster
Sage Copy Editor: Joyce Kuhn
Sage Typesetter: Janelle LeMaster

Contents

Acknowledgments

The authors extend special thanks to Patricia Harmon for sharing her vast experience in supervising interview surveys, and for providing a multitude of "real-world" survey material from which many of the examples in this book were derived. Thanks are also extended to Robert Haile, Dr.Ph., for permission to include and adapt questionnaire and training materials from his projects, particularly the Kaiser/UCLA Sigmoidoscopy-Based Case-Conrol Study of Colon Polyps (Sigmoid Study), and to Barbara Vickrey, M.D., M.P.H. for permission to adapt material for study exercises related to epilepsy. Thanks also go to the Center For Survey Research of UNLV and the State of Nevada Nuclear Waste Office for materials that were used as illustrations and examples.

The authors would also like to express their appreciation to C. Deborah Laughton of Sage Publications and to Arlene Fink, Ph.D. for their patience and encouragement; several anonymous reviewers whose suggestions were very helpful in revisions of the manuscript; and Management Assistants, Veona Hunsinger and Susie LaFrentz, of the Sociology Department at UNLV, who were very helpful in the preparation phase of the manuscript.

How to Conduct Interviews by Telephone and In Person: Learning Objectives

The aim of this book is to guide the reader in the preparation and administration of survey interviews both by telephone and in person. Its specific objectives are to prepare the reader to:

- Choose the most appropriate interview mode (telephone or in person) for specific surveys

- Write interview questions with structured interviewer instructions

- Employ appropriate question-writing techniques based on whether the interview will be done by telephone or in person

- Construct useful visual aids

- Organize a flowing interview script that considers possible question order effects

- Write an informative introductory statement

- Write a preletter

- Write a script for a precall

- Design an eligibility screen

- Write and appropriately place transition statements

- Write a job description for an interviewer

- Develop an interviewer training manual

- Design an interviewer training session

- Describe the role of a supervisor

1 Overview of Telephone and In-Person Interviews

A survey interview is a purposeful conversation in which one person asks prepared questions (the interviewer) and another answers them (the respondent). It is a directed conversation, the purpose of which is to gather information by means of administering the same set of questions in a consistent way to all selected respondents. These respondents presumably are representative of the population of interest, or **target population**.

The interview is a key data-collection tool for conducting surveys. A **data-collection tool** is a structured method of obtaining information about selected characteristics, or **variables**, in a target population. Depending on the topic of the survey, the variables may include specific knowledge, attitudes, and behaviors prevalent among the members of the population. The ultimate goal of the survey is to produce quantifiable measures of these variables that can be statistically analyzed to generate reliable observations. This is best done using a standardized questionnaire.

Standardized questionnaires are designed to reduce error that could be attributed to the interviewer. This is accomplished by scripting the question format and question order, defining in detail how the interviewer is to move through the questionnaire, and defining how the interviewer is to respond to questions or comments from the respondent. Standardization presumably leaves nothing to chance: Interviewers are instructed to be robotic when administering the instrument; however, they are also charged with the task of preventing the respondent from refusing to respond or prematurely terminating the interview. This is done by keeping the interview at a "conversational" level yet at the same time guiding the respondent along a prescribed path of questions and response alternatives.

Not many can fulfill this dual role of maintaining rapport through conversation while also performing a restricted, uniform, instrumental task. This makes interviewing a complex and demanding task. One can design the most technically proficient interview format, but if the interviewing is poorly done, the validity of the results can be severely compromised. The task of interviewing is made easier with properly designed questions (discussed in Chapter 2) and with adequate training and supervision (covered in Chapter 3).

Advantages and Disadvantages of Using Survey Interviews

Although surveys done by interview are usually more expensive, surveyors will choose them over self-administered questionnaires because of the role the interviewer can play in enhancing respondent participation, guiding the questioning, answering the respondent's questions, and clarifying the meaning of responses. In self-administered questionnaires, the respondent personally reads the questions and marks response options; the interviewer is not present to probe, clarify, and motivate the respondent to complete the questionnaire. Also, the surveyor loses control of the response pattern because the mailed questionnaire can be answered in any question sequence and by someone other than the selected respondent.

Another drawback of using self-administered questionnaires, whether mailed or distributed in a group setting, is their reliance on self-selected samples; that is, although the sample may be systematically determined, only those respondents personally motivated to complete and return the questionnaire will be heard from. Such samples often do not meet the criterion of representativeness—that is, the survey results obtained from the sample cannot be generalized to the target population. Interview samples are systematically determined and selected respondents are not in a position to "throw away" the questionnaire. Once contacted, they are more likely to participate in an interview survey (see **How to Sample in Surveys,** Vol. 6 in this series, for an in-depth discussion of sample selection).

IN-PERSON INTERVIEWING

One-on-one, in-person interviews have advantages over telephone interviews in terms of fewer limitations on the types and length of questioning and in the ability to use visual aids. Examples of locations for one-on-one interviews are the respondent's home, workplace, school, or the survey office, to name a few. Even though this form of interviewing is hampered by higher field costs, increased resistance on the part of respondents to invite strangers into their homes, and difficulty obtaining permission from management to conduct interviews in the workplace, it is regarded by researchers as one of the best ways to obtain detailed data. Other types of interview settings are possible:

- *Intercept interviews*, in which potential respondents are "intercepted" during an activity, such as shopping at a mall and questioned briefly on the spot
- *Group interviews*, in which formal techniques are used to question several people at the same time

This book discusses one-on-one, in-person interviews only. The reader is referred to Morgan (1993) and Frey and Fontana (1991) for a discussion of group interviewing.

TELEPHONE INTERVIEWING

Telephone interviewing is an increasingly popular means of conducting survey research because not only does almost everyone have a telephone but sampling techniques, such as **random digit dialing (RDD)**, make it easier to access unlisted and new numbers. Other reasons why telephone interviewing is being used more are its cost-efficiency and speed of data collection.

When used to survey the general population, as in national Gallup polls, telephone surveys also have the advantage of excellent sample coverage and generally high response rates. When telephone surveys are done for formal research, centralized calling units are often created. In such a unit, all interviewers contact respondents from specially equipped calling stations rather than calling from their own homes or private offices. The stations may employ special telephone equipment, such as listening devices and recording equipment.

Under such conditions, the telephone interview has its greatest advantage—the opportunity for quality control— because a supervisor (a person responsible for monitoring quality of interviewing) can observe interviews as they take place and give immediate feedback. In some **computer-assisted telephone interviewing (CATI)** operations, a supervisor can monitor an interview by listening from another station while the interview is being conducted. This is permissible if the interviewer informs the respondent that a supervisor may be listening to the interview for monitoring and quality control purposes. If the respondent agrees to continue the interview with full knowledge that a third party may possibly listen in on the conversation, then legal requirements of disclosure have been satisfied.

Of course, not all surveys are conducted as part of a sophisticated, well-funded research project. Smaller surveys (and many large ones) still use the paper-and-pencil method. Also, the creation of a central calling unit is not always possible. Other procedures can be developed. For example, an organization doing a small survey with limited resources can choose to have interviewers make calls from their homes and reimburse the charges. However, such a survey can also be able to imitate the central calling unit concept if office space with telephones can be made available so a supervisor can stand by.

Technological Advances in Interviewing

Recent technological developments have made interviewing, particularly by telephone, more feasible and more reliable.

The usual method for administering a questionnaire and recording responses is the "paper-and-pencil" method: Questions are read from a printed questionnaire in a prescribed sequence, and answers are recorded directly onto the questionnaire or code sheet. One of the problems associated with this method is human error on the part of the interviewer. For example, the interviewer may inadvertently overlook a question, ask questions in the wrong order, or accept an answer that is inconsistent with the range of response alternatives.

The integration of the computer into data gathering has improved the level of data quality for both telephone and in-person interviewing. For example, an organization with affiliates in several locations, such as the American Cancer Society, might find it worthwhile to equip each site with computers and software to standardize question asking for a large national survey. Computer-assisted telephone interviewing (CATI) and **computer-assisted personal interviewing (CAPI)** make it possible for the interview to be completed with fewer problems of interviewer error (for a fairly extensive discussion of computer-assisted survey techniques, see Frey, 1989).

The computer-assisted techniques direct the flow of each interview and automatically control the sequence of questions. Discrepancies in response can even be detected from one question to another. Also, these systems can be programmed to generate telephone numbers to call and to process data almost immediately. Although their use results in greater efficiency of administration, especially in larger surveys, and enhanced quality control, CATI and CAPI require considerable investment in hardware and presurvey programming and therefore may not lower a survey's overall cost. Which system to use is among the many decisions a surveyor must make when preparing an interview survey. The first and more basic decision required is whether to do the interviews by telephone or in person. Before delving into the specific issues associated with telephone and in-person interviewing, it is appropriate to discuss survey administration.

Survey Administration

Sometimes, surveyors pay little or no attention to the organizational or administrative details of the survey, assuming that these details will take care of themselves and that administration is not as important as data gathering. However, administration is a factor in **quality control** and therefore a factor in data quality. Quality control refers to procedures that organize and monitor survey activities for optimal results. For example, coordinating field operations, managing survey center operations, controlling sample selection, gaining productivity from interviewers, and properly implementing the survey according to plan are important administrative functions. If done properly, these procedures contribute to the overall quality of the data. Administrative procedures are developed in accordance with the **design** of the survey and its budget. Design refers to the overall plan for carrying out the following:

- How respondents will be sampled
- How many respondents need to be interviewed (see **How to Sample in Surveys,** Vol. 6 in this series)
- Complexity and length of questionnaire demanded by survey topic

- Interview mode
- How data will be analyzed (use of computer program or an outside consultant)

Once the design of the survey is determined and budgetary constraints are known, an administrative framework to handle implementation of this design can be conceptualized that includes the following:

- Number of interviewers needed and intensity of training required to meet sampling requirements
- Type and amount of supervision needed based on questionnaire complexity and interview mode
- Other personnel needed (clerks, data entry personnel, statistical experts) to handle data volume
- Facilities needed to house operations, including office equipment and storage space
- Amounts of supplies to stock (paper, pens, notepads, etc.)

After setting up the framework, administrative procedures that monitor and ensure the quality of the flow of data from interview through data analysis can be implemented. For example, a foundation that funds fellowships to support the development of academic researchers decides to do a survey to determine how many award recipients actually stay in academics (vs. going into industry). The foundation wishes to survey recipients over the past 10 years, or 150 fellows. The questionnaire will be simple (about five questions related to career development and current position) and administered by telephone. However, many addresses and phone numbers are outdated, but a complete list of names does exist. An appropriate administrative framework might include the following:

- Two part-time interviewers
- One part-time supervisor to stand by during interviews and do quality checks on completed surveys
- One part-time assistant to search for new telephone numbers of former fellows by calling the fellows' former institutions, scanning databases for recent publications (these list the author's affiliation), and using other location strategies. This duty could also be carried out by interviewers to keep personnel to a minimum.
- One or two calling stations, depending on whether both interviewers will be phoning at the same time
- A drawer in a filing cabinet to hold up to 150 interviews, even though not all fellows will be found and interviewed
- One part-time data enterer
- Several reams of paper, pencils, and notepads

ADMINISTRATIVE PLAN

The first step is to draft and implement an **administrative plan,** which defines the sequence of tasks, the timetable and person(s) having responsibility for these tasks, and all of the activities required as part of each larger task (e.g., sampling or questionnaire design). It is helpful to create a flowchart of major tasks in sequence, with the most important properly designated and singled out. That is, some tasks must be completed before any others can be carried out. For example, you cannot interview without the questionnaire. This technique is similar to the critical path method used in business and government for event planning.

ACTIVITY CHECKLIST

Another necessary administrative component is the **activity checklist.** This is an enumeration of all the major and minor tasks that must be completed. Each task is the assigned responsibility of a member of the research team and is given a scheduled completion date. All tasks should have a means of being monitored because many tasks are being carried out simultaneously. An activity checklist is especially helpful to survey administrators regarding distribution of the sample, determination of the status of each call or contact, and calculation of expense (i.e., budget).

An example of the activity checklist for a telephone survey follows. A similar format can be used for the in-person survey.

Activity Checklist

✓ **Establish project timetable.**

1. Interview training
2. Sample selection
3. Interviewing begins
4. Report due
5. Other _____

✓ **Set up survey facility.**

1. Reserved for calling
2. Equipment working
3. CATI system programmed

✓ Fill personnel requirements.

1. Operations supervisor(s)
2. Interviewers
3. Coder(s)/data entry
4. Programmer
5. Sample control person
6. CATI supervisor
7. Other _____

✓ Prepare budget.

1. Contract amount
2. Accounts and budget control procedure
3. Itemization
4. Other _____

✓ Select and train interviewers.

1. Recruiting
2. Training materials
3. Training scheduled
4. Employment contract
   - Employment referral form
   - Employee time card
   - W-4 form
   - Time sheet
5. Training completed

✓ Obtain supplies.

1. Phone books, if necessary
2. Pencils
3. Stapler
4. Other _____

✓ Determine sampling and calling.

1. Exchange/area proportions
2. Random selection of numbers
3. Number assignment forms
4. Call record form
5. Interviewer calling summary
6. Preletter, if necessary
7. Within-household selection procedure
8. Result codes
9. Codebook

✓ Develop questionnaire.

1. Pretest
2. Final draft
3. Printed and assembled
4. Assignment form
5. Probe instructions
6. Standardized responses to respondent questions

✓ Analyze data.

1. Codebook
2. Item codes
3. Coding form
4. Computer program
5. Computer accounts

✓ Disseminate survey information.

1. Formal report
2. Internal notification (e.g., department)
3. Press release or other publicity

Administration makes its major contribution to quality control and error reduction through continuous internal monitoring of the data collection process. This involves record keeping and close supervision. Interviewers must keep in continuous contact with their field supervisor, which means filing completed interviews or call summaries on a daily basis. This work is reviewed for accuracy and productivity. Every completed questionnaire must be edited and reviewed before being passed on to the data entry staff. Validation of at least 10% of completed interviews is implemented randomly; that is, all interviewers will have some of their interviews confirmed as to time and location.

Response rates, including refusals and partial completions, are monitored on a daily basis to assess the quality of the sample. Refusals and partial completions along with accuracy measures in the completion of the questionnaire become the basis on which to evaluate the performance of interviewers. Those who have the highest refusal rates or who seem to generate the same answer patterns (e.g., all respondents interviewed by "Jane" fall into the same category on most questions) or have a problem recording responses correctly and legibly may require additional training or should be terminated.

Replacement telephone numbers or field addresses are only assigned when the originally selected respondent has been determined to be ineligible or that respondent has been impossible to reach despite repeated callbacks because of a continuous no answer/answering machine or busy signal. In the latter case, that respondent remains "in sample" as a counted eligible respondent and becomes a part of the calculation of the actual response rate for the survey.

Attentive administration results in improved quality control, which means reduced systematic nonsampling and sampling error. Administration also means a careful and continuous assessment of the project's resource consumption. It is the rare project that is not limited by time, money, labor pool skills, and facilities. Tracking the budget is definitely a factor in quality control.

Determining the Sample

A **sample** is a portion or subset of the population the surveyor is interested in interviewing and is drawn when it is impractical to survey everyone in the population. A good sample is a miniature version of the population—just like it, only smaller.

Most surveys of special subpopulations use some kind of a list, or **sampling frame,** from which to draw a sample of potential interview respondents. For example, a school may use a roster of names and telephone numbers of first-graders' parents from which to randomly select respondents to call regarding their feelings about a new reading program. A research study may use medical records from the offices of selected lung specialists to identify asthma patients and record names and telephone numbers onto a list from which to sample.

However, lists are only one of the ways a sample can be obtained. A company wishing to survey employees regarding job satisfaction could randomly select office numbers and then randomly select desks within those offices without regard for who sits at them. The persons occupying the chosen desks comprise the sample. As long as everyone in the company has a desk, each person has an equal chance of being chosen.

Sampling is a complex topic worth understanding thoroughly when conducting any survey, whether by interview or otherwise. It is beyond the scope of this book to discuss sampling in detail, especially as the principles of sound sampling are not unique to interview surveys (see **How to Sample in Surveys,** Vol. 6 in this series, for a detailed discussion of sampling issues and techniques). There are, however, two sampling methods that are particularly relevant to telephone and in-person surveys of the general population: These are, respectively, random digit dialing (RDD) and area probability sampling. Both techniques eliminate the need for a list as possible respondents are chosen by randomly generating a telephone number or randomly choosing a housing unit within a geographic area. The person responding to the contact attempt is usually interviewed, if found eligible and willing, during that contact.

RANDOM DIGIT DIALING

For telephone surveys, access to the general population is enhanced by the use of *random digit dialing (RDD)*. This procedure is designed to overcome problems of sampling from telephone directories, which is the usual sampling frame for telephone surveys. Directories are often inaccurate and out-of-date. They are also incomplete because of unlisted numbers. As many as 60% or more of all telephone numbers are unlisted in some urban areas. RDD has overcome these flaws and thus made telephone interviewing a much more feasible option than it once was.

The first step in using RDD is to determine what three-digit exchanges (e.g., 458, 392) are in use in the target area (the geographic area within which the survey is to be conducted) and what blocks of 1000 or four-digit numbers are assigned. This information can be obtained by consulting the telephone directories that cover the target area or by contacting the local telephone company. If this information is not available from telephone directories or telephone companies, it is possible to purchase tapes from ITT listing central offices and numbers in use, but these are often out-of-date and inaccurate.

From this information, the surveyor can build unique seven-digit numbers efficiently. If the 739 exchange has residential numbers assigned between 2000 and 5000, the surveyor will draw a four-digit number randomly, within that range, usually via a computer program that generates listings of random numbers.

The four-digit number is then matched with the exchange. The combined number of 739-3467, for example, could be a number that one might have found in the directory, but it could also be a new number not yet listed or an unlisted number. That number is called. It is possible that the selected number will turn out to be a commercial setting or represent a household outside the target area. These possibilities mean that several calls may be made before an eligible respondent is reached. RDD and other improved telephone sampling techniques are reviewed in Frey (1989).

AREA PROBABILITY SAMPLING

A very useful strategy for household sampling because it can be applied to any population that can be defined geographically is what is termed **area probability sampling.** People living in a neighborhood, city, or country can be sampled this way. The basic concept is to divide the target area into exhaustive, mutually exclusive subareas with identifiable boundaries from which a sample is randomly drawn. Then, a list is made of housing units in each of these subareas, and a sample of these is drawn.

All of the people in selected housing units may be included in the sample, or they may be listed and sampled separately. This technique can be used both for sparsely populated rural areas and for downtown areas in large cities or any other geographic unit.

SAMPLE COVERAGE

When some of your target population cannot be reached by the interview mode you are using, data quality might be compromised by incomplete **sample coverage.** Any type of random sampling technique will overlook, for example, those who are homeless or live in cars or RVs, converted garages, or other nontraditional household settings. If these people are different from those you *can* reach in a way that is relevant to the survey objectives, your results will be biased (see Example 1.1). The incorrect conclusions you may draw are said to be due to "sampling error."

EXAMPLE 1.1
Compromised Sample Coverage

You are conducting a survey to determine levels of posttraumatic stress among survivors of a serious earthquake. Two weeks after the quake you can reach many survivors by telephone because lines have been restored and no longer need to be kept open for disaster procedures. However, the hardest hit victims are still living in tents and shelters without telephone service. If you survey by telephone only, you will lose their responses and hence will be omitting information about the stress manifestations of the hardest hit victims, which are likely to be different from those of victims still residing in their homes. Thus, your data will be incomplete and probably biased toward lower levels of posttraumatic stress than are actually being experienced in the population of earthquake survivors.

When interviewing special subpopulations, sample coverage must be considered in the context of the specific survey, its objectives, and target population. For surveys of the general population, however, random digit dialing and area probability sampling have overcome most sample coverage problems.

Deciding whether to interview by telephone or in person requires logistic and data quality considerations.

Logistics

It is not always obvious whether interviews should be done by telephone or in person for a particular survey. To decide which interview mode to use, start by considering three questions regarding the logistics of conducting the survey:

- What resources, including funding, personnel, time, and facilities, are available?
- What are the characteristics of the target population?
- What are the survey objectives?

AVAILABILITY OF RESOURCES

Funds

The availability of funds is often a powerful factor in determining how a survey will be conducted and may demand the less expensive interview mode from the start. When comparing telephone versus in-person interviews of the general public, the in-person mode is almost always more expensive. Because of the travel involved and because fewer interviews can be done in a given amount of time than by telephone, more and better-skilled interviewers and supervisors to monitor them are required. For these and other reasons, large-scale, in-person interviewing can be an extremely costly endeavor.

Surveys of smaller target groups using the in-person interview mode will usually also turn out to be more expensive but not always. Other resources, such as personnel, time for implementation, and facilities, need to be considered.

Personnel

Core personnel are interviewers to conduct interviews, supervisors to monitor the quality of interviewing, and any support staff (depending on the size of the survey) to handle administrative tasks, such as word processing, filing, and answering telephones. Depending on the nature and size of the survey, there may be an assortment of other personnel needed to run the survey, analyze findings, and locate difficult-to-reach respondents.

If the survey requires travel (as opposed to doing in-person interviews on-site, such as interviewing students at school), it is likely to require more personnel than a telephone survey. It may also be necessary to send more than one interviewer to a location where safety is a concern. This is true for some neighborhoods or locations where a potential threat exists. Also, because in-person interviews have more pitfalls for interviewers (discussed in a later chapter), more training will probably be required, and more supervisors may be needed.

Time

In-person interviewing will also usually take more time, again because of the travel factor. Using the telephone, a single interviewer can reach a large number of people over a wide geographic area in a short amount of time. Telephone interviews are often counted in numbers completed per hour. In-person interviews are more likely to be counted in numbers completed per day or per week, but if they are done on-site, as at a school, time is not as much of an issue.

Facilities

Facilities include space to house the survey's activities and equipment to carry out its functions. If you decide to set up a central calling unit so as to optimally supervise telephone interviewing, the cost of renting space and setting up calling stations with appropriate equipment may be more than sending interviewers to respondent's homes. If sufficient telephone equipment is available at your organization, say, during off hours (evenings and weekends), it will probably be cheaper to interview by telephone.

Inviting respondents to come to your facility for the interview is another possibility, although you might get a higher refusal rate if people have to go out of their way to participate in the survey. Sometimes, though, there is no other way to conduct the survey—for example, if respondents are asked to react to a nontransportable visual, like a museum display.

If a survey is large enough to consider implementing computer-assisted interviewing, facility costs (also personnel and training costs) go up.

CALCULATING THE COST OF INTERVIEWING

To determine which interview mode would cost you more to use, make a list of the resources you have available and those you would need to obtain for each interview mode and compare the costs.

EXAMPLE 1.2
Evaluating Resources to Compare Costs of Telephone Versus In-Person Interviewing

You work for a private women's college that is considering going coed to increase enrollment. You are afraid that enrollment could actually decline, however, if current students vehemently oppose going coed and drop out. You decide to interview a sample of current students to assess their views. No one currently on staff has ever conducted a survey before, but a reliable group of volunteer alumnae do regular telephone work for organizing campus events. You have very little money to conduct the study. You are also pressed for time because you need to know whether you are going to go coed in time for the print deadline of the application brochure.

You have an office available, equipped with several desks and telephones, where interviews could be done by telephone after 5 p.m. and on weekends. You also have access to a language lab that has private booths where you could conduct in-person interviews during the day. However, it is only available from 3 p.m. to 6 p.m. on weekdays, and your alumna volunteers are professionals who are not available during those hours. They also have no experience with in-person interviewing, so you would have to hire and train interviewers. You plan to design the questionnaire yourself and then hire a statistics student to do your analysis. You will get training to provide supervision yourself. You make a list of your resources:

Resource	By Telephone	In Person
Funding	Minimal funds available: Need to cover the cost of telephone bills (a few long-distance calls are expected), printing of questionnaires and training materials, and salary for the data analyst Alumnae will do interviews without compensation; however, a small stipend may be provided.	Minimal funds available: Need to cover interviewer salaries, printing of questionnaires and training materials, and data analyst salary; no travel costs if interviews are done in language lab
Personnel	Alumnae with telephoning experience are available to conduct telephone interviews evenings and weekends. They need to be trained in interviewing skills.	No existing personnel can do the job. Must recruit, screen, hire, and train interviewers
Time	Limited: If done by telephone, training can commence as soon as training materials are prepared.	Limited: More time will be needed than for the telephone interview to recruit and hire interviewers. Developing the training materials will take longer as will training.
Facilities	An office with telephones is available after hours and on weekends, which could constitute a calling unit where interviews could be listened to by a supervisor in the background.	The language lab provides a private setting for interviews from 3 p.m. to 6 p.m. each day.

Analysis of Survey Mode Options: Telephone Versus In Person

Telephone: Many of the resources to set up for telephone interviews are available. Costs can be kept low because most students live locally, avoiding the cost of long-distance calls, and a volunteer labor pool is available, except for the data analyst. There are essentially no costs for facilities, and setup would take very little time because interviewers need not be located. An up-to-date list of student names and telephone numbers should be available from the main office, making it easy to randomly select respondents and to use the telephone to reach them.

In Person: This survey is more expensive to do because of personnel costs for finding and training interviewers. It would also require more time to do the hiring and training. If you call students to arrange appointments at the language lab, more money and time will be required because recruiting and interviewing are separate, as opposed to immediate interviewing if done by phone. If you sample from classrooms (randomly choosing classes, and then students within classes), money, time, and personnel will be needed to make the selections and orchestrate the scheduling of interviews.

This survey is clearly more expensive to do in person. However, you have not yet considered whether doing the interviews by telephone will give you less useful data than doing them in person.

In a later section, a data quality checklist will help you focus on issues as they relate to interview mode. If money and time are so tight that you cannot do the interview in person, you still need to review the checklist. Otherwise, you will not understand the limitations within which to interpret your survey's results.

CHARACTERISTICS OF THE TARGET POPULATION

The population of interest may dictate the mode of interview that is most likely to get results. Access to respondents in some target groups may be impossible by one mode or the other. If members of the target group are homeless, for example, logistically speaking, telephone interviews cannot even be considered. If the target group is widely dispersed geographically, in-person interviewing may be logistically impractical.

Other considerations in terms of target group characteristics are whether the overall education level and language skills are sufficient to allow comprehension of questions spoken over the telephone (which are easier to simplify in person) and whether fear for personal safety in a particular group (e.g., women living alone) would make it inappropriate to interview in the home. Many target group considerations will not rule out an interview mode completely but may have an impact on data quality, as when too many respondents refuse to participate because they are afraid to let an interviewer come to the home. The details of data quality considerations may be reviewed using the checklist provided later in this chapter.

SURVEY OBJECTIVES

The objectives of a particular survey may be more difficult to satisfy with one of the interview modes. For example, if the survey has objectives requiring direct observation of respondents' characteristics, it cannot be done by telephone. A psychological survey might have the following among its objectives: to compare consistency of body language cues with verbal responses to questions about drug use. Because body language cues must be observed, the survey has to be done in person.

To address the objective of finding out whether the local library is open at the right times for potential users to have access, the entire interview might consist of only three or four questions and take 5 minutes to complete. In this case, it would be logistically impractical to drive to respondents' homes for a 5-minute interview, so you would conduct your survey by telephone.

Data Quality

Logistic considerations will sometimes rule out an interview mode at the outset. Money or time availability may be severely restrictive, respondents may be absolutely inaccessible, or survey objectives may be impossible to meet by one mode or the other. Very often, however, the decision will require some thought. Logistic considerations must be weighed against a checklist of considerations concerning the quality of the data generated by one mode versus the other. Data quality involves the following:

- *Validity:* The accuracy with which the survey measures what it is supposed to
- *Reliability:* The precision, or consistency, of measurements from interview to interview of the data collected by each interview mode
- *Generalizability:* The extent to which conclusions about a sample are true about the entire population (also called external validity)

When logistics require choosing the less informative interview mode, the limitations of the data need to be understood for optimal interpretation. For example, if you were forced to do a survey by telephone knowing that generalizability might be compromised because some members of your target population were unreachable by telephone, you must qualify the conclusions you draw from your data. The checklist must therefore still be reviewed.

Data Quality Considerations Checklist

THE SAMPLE

✓ **Sample coverage:** Ability of a survey to reach all eligible respondents.

✓ **Response rate:** Degree to which the surveyor is successful in obtaining cooperation from all eligible respondents in a sample—that is, how often they are reached and agree to participate. The most informative way to calculate the response rate is to divide the number of completed interviews by the number of eligible respondents in the sample. When nonrespondents and respondents differ on important factors (e.g., education level), nonresponse bias is introduced. Also, if the response rate is low, the sample may become too small to produce precise and reliable findings.

✓ **Confidentiality:** Assurance given respondents that identifying information known about them (e.g., name, telephone number, and address) will not be revealed in any way. The issue with confidentiality is the ability to convince respondents that their identity can and will be kept secret. When respondents fear that confidentiality cannot be ensured, response rates may be lower.

  ■ *Comment:* Problems with sample coverage and response rates affect the generalizability of a survey's findings because those who are interviewed may be different from those who are not.

THE INTERVIEWER

✓ **Interviewer effects:** Interviewer behaviors and characteristics that bias the respondent's answers. Interviewers may interject their own opinions into the interview conversation, show approval or disapproval with tone of voice or facial expression, or present questions using their own words instead of those printed on the questionnaire.

✓ **Clarifications:** Done by interviewers when a respondent has not understood the question or the answer is not complete or is imprecise.

✓ **Ability to probe:** Technique used to get more information when a response is unclear or incomplete. Probes include simple gestures, such as nodding or saying "uh-huh," and neutral questions like "Could you tell me more about that?" to motivate the respondent to say more.

■ *Comment:* The interviewer can positively or negatively influence validity and reliability of questionnaire responses. Validity and reliability are compromised if the interviewer changes the meaning of questions or responses through biased interviewing technique, or insufficient skills in clarifying and probing. When the interviewer is skilled in these techniques, questioning is standardized, making responses more comparable from one respondent to the next. Data quality is thus enhanced.

THE QUESTIONS

✓ **Sensitive questions:** Ones that a respondent may be uncomfortable answering. Questions about finances, sexuality, illegal behavior (e.g., drug use), or embarrassing events (e.g., filing bankruptcy or being arrested) may be considered "sensitive" by respondents.

✓ **Complex questions:** Ones that require lengthy explanations or numerous response categories.

✓ **Open-ended questions:** Ones that do not offer response choices. Respondents are completely free to frame their answer.

✓ **Questions using visual aids:** Ones that involve visual tools to help respondents understand questions and answer them accurately. Visual aids, such as charts, maps, and lists, are rarely used for telephone interviews but are a valuable tool for in-person surveys.

- *Comment:* Answers to sensitive, complex, and open-ended questions may compromise validity and reliability if not asked in a way that ensures respondent comprehension. Visual aids and certain question-writing techniques can simplify questions and response options to enhance comprehension.

THE RESPONSES

✓ **Item nonresponse:** Frequency with which a given item simply is not answered, or the answer is uninformative, such as "don't know" or "no opinion," or may not seem to make sense. Item nonresponse can be due to imprecise question wording, causing respondents difficulty in understanding, or they may refuse to answer because the question is sensitive or embarrassing. Alternatively, an item may be inadvertently skipped or incorrectly recorded by the interviewer.

✓ **Socially desirable responses:** Answers that respondents may give because of a belief that the response is what they "should" believe rather than what they actually do believe. For example, respondents who are smokers might respond favorably to limiting smoking in public places because smoking is viewed unfavorably among their peers. However, the respondents may actually find the restrictions annoying. Similarly, white respondents may give responses favorable to racial integration to an African American interviewer but actually resent integration measures. The latter is an example of a socially desirable response due to interviewer effect.

✓ **Questionnaire length:** Time required to ask all of the questions. Some topics can be covered in a few minutes with a small number of simple questions. Others require lengthy questioning using special procedures to present complex and sensitive items. Questionnaire length deserves consideration because lengthy interviews may result in respondent and interviewer fatigue. Fatigue can lead to less thoughtful responses or incomplete interviews.

■ *Comment:* Validity is compromised when respondents do not answer questions, give responses that do not reflect their true feelings to be "socially" acceptable, or stop answering thoughtfully because an interview is too long.

SAMPLE COVERAGE

Sample coverage is usually good with either interview mode, unless a specific target population as a whole or a certain group of people is difficult to reach by one mode or the other. This is discussed in detail in an earlier section of this chapter.

RESPONSE RATE

The degree to which cooperation is obtained from all eligible respondents in a sample is its **response rate.** The rate at which persons agree to be interviewed is influenced by many factors, including sampling technique, topic of survey, and how appealing the survey sounds during the introduction. No particular rate is accepted as standard, but if rates of 70% to 80% are achieved, one can feel comfortable with analyses based on the data. Every effort should be made to achieve this rate for the general population; lower rates may be acceptable for specialized, homogeneous populations.

Response rates are subject to significant variation in how they are calculated. The correct rate is generally a reflection of how successful the surveyor is in obtaining cooperation from all of the eligible respondents. It is the measure of the effectiveness of data collection and is determined as follows:

Response Rate = Completed interviews/
Number in sample eligible.

Eligible respondents include completed interviews, refusals, partial completions, those with answering machines or who never answered, and numbers where a language barrier existed. Ineligible respondents are those who did not have a household member with the defining characteristic for inclusion, such as "adult over the age of 18" or "someone currently working full-time." Even if a household is never contacted, it is still considered eligible because there was no substantial evidence to eliminate it from the sampling pool.

Response is harder to get these days. Just contacting a potential respondent by phone is becoming increasingly difficult because of technological barriers, such as the answering machine and call waiting. Busy schedules, a desire for privacy, and fear for personal safety also make it difficult to obtain compliance. Surveyors must pay attention to these factors and address them.

At least five or six callbacks, or repeated attempts to reach a respondent, should be scheduled for telephone surveys—even more than that if it looks as if there is going to be some difficulty obtaining an adequate response rate. Field costs should include a budget for callbacks or return contacts with in-person respondents. Given the fact that respondents are harder to reach today than ever before, the surveyor could expect to make a callback or recontact in at least 50% of the sample cases. The denominator, or the definition of eligibility, is not consistently implemented in practice.

Often, survey research is reported with a response rate based on the ratio of completed interviews to refusals plus completions. This produces the "public relations" rate that makes the surveyor look good but is not an accurate record of response success. Response rates must be calculated at the end of each interview day and not at the end of the field phase of the survey.

The most revealing measure of a survey's success is the refusal rate or the number of eligible individuals who decide not to participate in the survey for one reason or another. Because refusals are known to be eligible, provisions must be made for refusal conversion. This is usually a task left to the most persuasive interviewers. When within-household selection techniques are used, the refusal could come at two points—with the person who is first contacted and with the selected eligible respondent.

In compiling the response summary for the study, each of these refusal points must be differentiated and included in the calculation. This will be important when refusal conversion, or convincing a person who previously refused to participate to do so, is attempted because the interviewer will need to know the exact status of the initial contact and who to try to contact when calling. Refusal rates are on the increase: 25% to 30% is not uncommon today. This, of course, creates concern about the representativeness of the sample. *With the use of sound sampling methods and systematic and persistent follow-up procedures, good response rates can be achieved for surveys using either telephone or in-person interviews.*

In some instances, the target group or survey content may lead to a poorer response rate by one interview mode or the other. Research has shown, for example, that so-called elite populations (people in socially elevated positions, such as lawyers and politicians) are more likely to participate in telephone interviews. Sensitive topics, however, are better approached in person.

CONFIDENTIALITY

Ensuring that respondents' **confidentiality** is protected is difficult in either interview mode but especially so with in-person interviews, where respondents are aware that the interviewer knows many of their identifying characteristics. These characteristics may include name, address, possibly telephone number, and personal appearance. Respondents' willingness to reveal information may hinge on their level of confidence that their identity will not be revealed.

Confidentiality can be compromised by validation callbacks ("checkup" calls to make sure the interview was actually done and not made up by the interviewer), which are often used in household and telephone surveys. These calls tell respondents that their name and telephone number have been passed on, even if only to the interviewer's supervisor.

It is not known how many respondents surveyed by telephone refuse to participate for privacy reasons. In surveys that employ RDD, the original identifying information is only a phone number as it is not necessary to have the respondent's name. The interviewer can assure respondents that their name is not known and will not be asked for. This may increase respondents' comfort level.

The possession of even the simplest of identifiers, such as a randomly generated telephone number, means that only **confidentiality**, not **anonymity**, can be ensured. Anonymity means that identifiers are not known; confidentiality means that no identifiers will be revealed. Confidentiality becomes a matter of trust—respondent of interviewer.

INTERVIEWER EFFECTS

The negative effects that an interviewer may have on the way a respondent answers a question are called **interviewer effects.** There are fewer negative effects for the telephone interview than for in-person questioning simply because visual cues, such as race or facial expressions, cannot be observed and so do not affect the response (Groves & Kahn, 1979). The interviewer can interject expectations and values into the interview exchange and can distort question wording, instruction guidelines, and probing guidelines, which can affect questionnaire completion.

Example 1.3 illustrates some instances of interviewer effects.

EXAMPLE 1.3
Interviewer Effects

1. *A question reads "What is your profession?"*

The interviewer ignores instructions to read questions verbatim and asks "What is your current job?" A teacher by profession might be currently working in a grocery store because of a teacher's strike and hence would answer the first question "teacher" and the second "grocery store clerk." The correct response is lost in this example, and what's worse, those who interpret the data will never know it unless the interview has been observed by a supervisor.

2. *A question reads "How did you find out about our program?" and has interviewer instructions "Do not read response options."*

The interviewer does not read the whole list of options out loud but begins offering some of them when the respondent hesitates. The respondent was about to say she was told about the program by a friend, but when the interviewer suggests a TV commercial, she says, "Oh, maybe I did see one." She does not go on to say that her friend's recommendation is what most motivated her to look into the program. The "correct" response has again been lost.

3. *A question reads "What is your opinion of how well the president is doing his job?"*

Although the interviewer's probing instructions are to remain neutral, say "uh-huh" and "please continue" to get a complete response, when the respondent says he is happy with the president's performance, the interviewer chuckles and asks, "Well, what about that illegal arms deal incident?" The chuckle tells the respondent that the interviewer disagrees with him, and the question about the arms deal takes the respondent in a direction he would not have chosen if left to respond on his own.

As previously stated, the centralized telephone interview can minimize biasing interviewer practices because of the close supervision that is possible. If, however, interviewers are allowed to make calls from their homes to save money, this advantage is lost. In-person interviews cannot be monitored constantly by a supervisor and are thus more vulnerable to interviewer effects. Interviewer body language, eye contact, and other nonverbal cues may influence respondents' answers. Standardized training of interviewers to follow the same protocol with each and every respondent is very important. The challenge is to follow the script but not to appear too mechanical about the questionnaire's administration because depersonalization contributes to nonresponse.

Clarifications and **probes** can be used most effectively in the in-person mode because of enhanced interviewer-respondent rapport and the ability to read a respondent's nonverbal cues indicating confusion or hesitation.

APPROPRIATE INTERVIEW MODE
FOR PARTICULAR QUESTIONS

Sensitive questions, or those that are potentially uncomfortable for the respondent to answer, can be asked in any type of survey because research shows no differences in response patterns by mode of inquiry (Frey, 1989). However, respondents are less likely to omit or give an incomplete answer to such items during the in-person interview simply because an interviewer is present to probe for a more complete response or to encourage respondents to answer the question despite its sensitive nature. Unfortunately, the potential for a socially desirable answer is also greater in the in-person interview. Telephone surveys show a higher rate of item nonresponse to sensitive questions (Frey, 1989).

Complex questions are also best asked in the in-person situation, mostly because visual aids can be used to help respondents understand the question or keep track of the response options. Respondents can get lost in the words over the telephone, losing track of multiple response categories or lengthy explanations. However, techniques such as funneling and split questions (described in Chapter 2) make it possible to ask more complex questions over the telephone. The advantage, however, still goes to the in-person interview, which also has the advantage when it comes to **open-ended questions.** Although these questions can be asked over the telephone, there is some evidence that they yield shorter, less detailed answers.

Visual aids are used almost exclusively with in-person interviews. They are difficult to use in telephone interviews because they need to be mailed in advance of the phone contact.

ITEM NONRESPONSE

Sources of **item nonresponse** include poorly worded or confusing questions and response categories, causing respondents difficulty in forming an opinion on the question. The expectations that an interviewer brings to the interview can also affect item nonresponse. For example, interviewers who believe that an item, such as a question on income or on abortion, is inappropriate or too difficult for a respondent will have higher item nonresponse rates. Interviewers who are less personable, more mechanical, and task oriented also will experience higher item nonresponse. In general, there is no appreciable difference in item nonresponse between telephone and in-person interviews, although nonresponse to the income question is higher for the telephone survey.

SOCIALLY DESIRABLE RESPONSES

Both types of interviews suffer from **socially desirable responses;** however, the problem is most prominent during in-person interviews. This is because the interviewer's sheer physical presence combined with visible characteristics, such as age or race, may influence the respondent's comments more than the removed voice on the telephone. The more personalized the interview, the greater the tendency for the respondent to answer in a manner perceived to be pleasing to the interviewer or to be generally expected within the social and political climate at the time.

QUESTIONNAIRE LENGTH

Questionnaire length is least restricted in the in-person interview. It is not uncommon to obtain interviews of 60 to 90 minutes in length. Over the longer interview time, interviewers can probe in greater depth, go further into establishing rapport, and thus be in a better position to ask sensitive questions. The development of new techniques in telephone questionnaire construction and interviewing procedure have made it possible to conduct somewhat lengthy interviews by telephone. Interviews of up to 50 minutes in length can be successfully conducted by telephone. Once the interviewer is past the introductory statements and into the first questions of the interview, length does not seem to be a problem. Respondents will complete the interview, apparently losing track of the time.

However, this does not mean that length is not an important consideration. After a certain time or number of questions, both interviewer and respondent fatigue affects the data quality. Answers may not be as thoughtful, and probing and clarifications on the part of the interviewer may be less thorough, causing data to be less complete.

Data Quality Summary

The weight given to the data quality considerations described in the preceding sections is influenced by the intended use of the data. Of course, high quality in terms of response accuracy and completeness and sample coverage is always a goal of any survey that is worth doing. However, the margin of error that can be tolerated will vary depending on how the data will be used.

If the study is only exploratory and the results are not a matter of "life and death," then the sampling/nonsampling error rate can be higher. For example, obtaining a population's general perception about social problems or community needs gives valuable information to politicians and policymakers, but sampling and interviewing technique may be compromised because a general sense is all that is required. However, if survey results will have a serious impact on jobs and appropriations, then these principles cannot be violated.

If the results of a knowledge, attitudes, and practices survey of smokers is going to be used to guide the planning of a larger-scale project, a certain margin of error may be tolerable. However, if data from such a survey will be used to determine national health education policy (which affects huge numbers of people and is hard to change once implemented), no detail of sampling, questionnaire construction, or questionnaire implementation (i.e., interviewing) can be left to chance.

There is no "right" way to conduct a survey. Modes other than the personal interview (e.g., mail surveys) can also be considered. Mode decisions will usually need to be made by weighing advantages and disadvantages of each mode in relation to the specific needs of the survey topic and target group. General advantages of telephone versus in-person interviews are summarized in the following table.

Data Quality Issue	Mode of Usual Advantage	Comments
Logistics		
Cost	Telephone	For most surveys, especially those of the general population, the telephone interview will be least expensive, requiring fewer personnel and less time.
Personnel	Telephone	
Time	Telephone	
The Sample		
Sample coverage	In person	Good sample coverage is usually possible with both modes. In-person interviewing provides better coverage with some special subpopulations.
Response rate	In person	Response rates are dropping for both modes. In-person interviews get somewhat higher rates.
Confidentiality	Telephone	Because a telephone interviewer usually knows less about the respondent, it is easier to ensure confidentiality. Neither mode can provide anonymity.
The Interviewer		
Interviewer effects	Telephone	Interviewer effects are lowest in the supervised centralized calling unit. They are also lower for telephone interviews in general because visible characteristics of the interviewer cannot influence respondent answers.
Clarifications	In person	Clarifications and probing are easier in person because the presence of the interviewer enhances rapport and allows observation of nonverbal cues indicating hesitation or confusion on the part of the respondent.
Ability to probe	In person	

$\rightarrow$

Data Quality Issue	Mode of Usual Advantage	Comments
Visual aids	In person	Visual aids enhance the in-person interview greatly. They are difficult to use in telephone interviews because they need to be mailed in advance and be available during the interview.
The Questions		
Sensitive questions	In person	In-person interviews get fewer omissions and incomplete responses for these. The reason is not known.
Open-ended questions	In person	More detailed answers may be given for these when asked in person.
The Responses		
Item nonresponse	Neither	Neither mode gets lower item nonresponse in general; nonresponse for the income question is higher by telephone.
Socially desirable responses	Telephone	These are more of a problem in person because the respondent may react to the interviewer's physical characteristics and may be more eager to please an interviewer who is physically present.
The Questionnaire		
Long questionnaires	In person	Longer interviews are possible in person because of increased rapport.

The most salient considerations for logistics and data quality in deciding interview mode will vary with the survey. Example 1.4 illustrates the decision process.

EXAMPLE 1.4
Survey Scenario

A survey of Los Angeles County (California) residents has the objective of describing the range of opinions on sensitive political issues, such as welfare reform, immigration laws, and health care policies. The nature of the questions is that they are complex and sensitive. The questionnaire is expected to be fairly long (at least 60 minutes). The county board of supervisors wants reliable data on which to base policy decisions and is providing reasonable funding.

The survey administrators realize that sensitive and complex questions are best asked in person using good visual aids, but they are worried that interviewer effects and social desirability will be a real problem. The political nature of the questions makes it likely that respondents will be looking for validation of their opinions from the interviewer, and their answers to the immigration questions may be influenced by the interviewer's race. The population of Los Angeles County is highly racially mixed, and the race match of the interviewer and respondent could have an effect. The length of the questionnaire favors doing it in person, although it is not impossible to do by telephone. There seems to be enough funding to do the interviews in person, but if done by telephone, a larger number of interviews can be done for the same amount of money. There is enough time to do the interview by either mode.

In weighing the considerations, the administrators decide that the validity of the more complex items will be compromised too much if they cannot use visual aids. There are too many complex items to address the problem with question-writing techniques that would allow the questions to be asked over the phone. Respondent fatigue would be inevitable. They also prefer the in-person mode because of the length of the questionnaire, which has not yet been developed. They prefer to leave open the option of a longer questionnaire, rather than having to cut items if the pilot test shows that the interview actually takes longer. They reason that only some of the questions might be affected by interviewer race and decide to assess the impact during a pretest.

They decide that a full week of training will be required to maximize interviewer skills. Special attention will be paid to providing practice in remaining neutral and reading questions as worded so as to minimize interviewer effects. Supervisors will accompany interviewers on occasional interviews to observe their techniques and give feedback.

Once preliminary decisions regarding the execution plan and interview mode of a survey have been made, the questionnaire can be designed. Questionnaire construction must take place with both the target group and the mode of interview in mind.

The next chapters discuss these issues.

2 Questionnaire Construction

The interview takes the form of a script. Its construction requires a marriage of art and science to achieve two primary goals: One is content that addresses the survey objectives; the other is smooth conversational flow. The interview script is composed of three important parts: introductory statement, eligibility screen, and questions. The introductory statement describes the survey and attempts to enlist participant cooperation, and the eligibility screen determines whether a potential respondent is suitable to be interviewed. Once respondents have been selected, the questions facilitate performing the real work of interviewing: data collection. A persuasive and informative introduction to the interview provides the means of obtaining the cooperation needed for successful data collection.

Introductory Statement

The crucial component of the interview for capturing the respondent's interest is the **introductory statement.** It must present information regarding the survey in conversational, nonthreatening language that convinces the respondent to participate. In the case of in-person interviewing, respondents have time to observe the interviewer and to listen to the introductory message. When a survey is presented by telephone, however, respondents have little time to make a decision. They must respond to an unanticipated, almost immediate request for an interview. In fact, prospective respondents for a telephone interview may not even hear the content of the introductory message or only hear selected components as they contemplate whether or not to agree to the interview. Thus, it is advisable to give each potential respondent as much time as possible to think about whether to participate.

The introductory statement, as short as it may be and with constraints of interviewer appearance and/or voice, has the major responsibility of building immediate rapport and trust with the respondent. A great deal of attention must be paid to the formulation of the introductory message. The following checklist can help guide the process.

Checklist for Preparing
Introductory Statements

✓ **Identify the person (use full name) making the contact.**

✓ **Identify the sponsor of the survey (e.g. foundation, university, marketing firm).**

✓ **Explain why the request is being made, including appropriate background on the survey, and what kind of information is sought.**

✓ **Verify that the right person, household, or telephone number has been reached.**

✓ **State any important conditions of the interview, such as level of confidentiality, voluntary nature of participation, approximate length of interview, and opportunity to ask questions.**

✓ **Describe any benefits of participation.**

✓ **Ask for permission to proceed with the questions.**

It is well documented that most terminations or refusals take place after the introduction but before the first question, so an interviewer will usually have an opportunity to describe the survey before the respondent decides whether or not to participate. The script for an introduction should first identify both the person making the contact and the sponsoring organization so as to establish the survey's credibility and then explain briefly why the request for an interview is being made. Respondents should not be wondering who is calling or what this is about when an identifying question using their name or phone number is asked. To avoid wasting both the respondent's and the interviewer's time, verification that the correct person or location has been reached should be made next. If the right person has been reached, brief details about the reason for the survey, its contents, and the conditions of the interview (e.g., confidentiality) and any benefits of participation should be given. These details offer the respondent the opportunity to make an informed decision about participation. Finally, a courteous request for permission to proceed makes the respondent feel respected and ensures voluntary participation.

There is some debate about just how much information should be given about the purpose of the survey. One view is that the respondent should be told as little as possible about the survey objectives to avoid biasing response patterns. For example, if respondents know that the survey is looking for the effects of alcohol in lowering the incidence of heart attacks, alcohol consumption might be reported differently than if they thought the subject was alcoholism.

Another view is that respondents should be well informed not only out of respect but to avoid possible accusations of malpractice or misconduct directed at the interviewer. The specific survey topic, its political context, the characteristics of the target population, and the cost in data quality (due to biased comments) must be considered in deciding how detailed the introductory statement can be.

Example 2.1 illustrates how introductory statements vary for telephone and in-person surveys.

EXAMPLE 2.1
Introductory Statements

Telephone

1. Hello. This is ___(full name of interviewer)___ calling from the Center for Survey Research at the University of Nevada, Las Vegas. We are conducting a survey of Clark County residents for their views on important issues facing the southern Nevada area. Is this the ___(respondent's last name)___ residence?

> (IF WRONG NUMBER OR INCORRECT LISTING, TERMINATE INTERVIEW BY SAYING SOMETHING LIKE "SORRY TO HAVE BOTHERED YOU"; IF CORRECT, PROCEED WITH REMAINDER OF INTRODUCTION)

Your number was selected at random from a local telephone directory, and your responses will be confidential.

> (INSERT SELECTION PROCEDURES FOR ELIGIBLE MEMBER OF HOUSEHOLD; REPEAT INTRODUCTION ABOUT PURPOSE OF STUDY)

May I begin asking some questions?

2. Hello. This is _____ calling from the Center for Survey Research at the University of Nevada, Las Vegas. We are conducting a survey of Clark County residents about community concerns. Before we continue, I need to know if I have dialed the correct number. Is this ___(number)___ ?

> (IF NO, END INTERVIEW BY SAYING "SORRY TO HAVE BOTHERED YOU"; IF YES, PROCEED WITH REMAINDER OF INTRODUCTION)

Your number was chosen for this survey by a random digit selection process. I would like to find out your opinions on some issues. May I proceed with the questions?

3.   Hello, my name is _____. I'm calling on behalf of Livingston Memorial Research Foundation. The Foundation is participating in a national study of the delivery of social services and their financing. Have I reached the Johnson residence? You should have received a brochure about the Livingston Social Services Programs within the past few days, and I'm calling to talk to you about your opinions of the programs. Your answers will be kept in the strictest confidence, and your name will not appear on the interview form. Do you have any questions? The interview will take about 5 minutes to complete. You may end the interview at any time. May I ask you questions?

The examples above illustrate how the components of the introductory statement might be synthesized for several different surveys. Although the flow is similar, the content and number of details (how names or phone numbers were acquired, whether length of interview is stated up front) varies with the nature of the survey and is a matter of the surveyor's judgment.

In Person

1.   Hello, my name is _____, and I represent the Democratic Party. We are doing a survey to get a feel for voter opinion on gun control legislation, and I am asking people in your neighborhood for their views. I will not ask your name or record any identifying characteristics about you on the survey form, except the neighborhood where the interview took place. Your participation will make your opinions heard in Washington. The survey takes about 7 minutes to complete. Do you have any questions? May I interview you?

(SHOW IDENTIFICATION IF NECESSARY)

2. My name is _____, and I am from UCLA. We are conducting a study of the health effects of environmental pollutants, funded by the National Institutes of Health. To learn about these effects we would like to ask you a number of questions about your health and daily activities. The information that you provide will be very important in helping us understand the relationship of the environment to health and will help to guide us in making decisions in these areas in the future. Your responses will be used for statistical purposes only and will not in any way be identified with you or members of your family. I'd like to begin by asking you some general questions about you and all other family members living in this house. May I continue?

Note that in both introductory statements the emphasis is on confidentiality information because the physical presence of the interviewer is more threatening to privacy than a request made over the phone.

These examples are intended as lead-in statements when the interview is to follow immediately. The respondent has been contacted either by telephone for an immediate interview or by a field interviewer who has knocked on the door or come to the workplace or similar setting. In the latter case, it is important that interviewers carry a letter of identification certifying that they represent a legitimate organization. Badges with the name of the interviewer and sponsoring organization clearly visible should be worn. Example 2.2 shows a letter of identification used in a survey on risk perception associated with the siting of a high-level nuclear waste repository.

EXAMPLE 2.2
Identification Letter

(LETTERHEAD - CENTER FOR SURVEY RESEARCH)

Date

Dear Clark County Resident:

This is to introduce _____ who is employed as an interviewer by the Center for Survey Research at the University of Nevada, Las Vegas. The interviewer will be asking several questions as part of a survey of Clark County residents on your attitudes and perceptions associated with various community issues and problems, including the proposed repository at Yucca Mountain. Your responses will be confidential. If you have questions or wish to verify the research, please feel free to call me or a field supervisor at 555-1234. Thank you for your help.

Sincerely,

James H. Frey, Ph.D.
Project Director

The message of this letter contains a statement of the survey purpose, an affirmation of confidentiality, and a telephone number the respondent can call to verify that the survey is genuine.

Advance Letters and Precalls

Interviews do not have to immediately follow the introduction. They can also be introduced by an **advance letter** (using a sampling list with addresses, if available) or a telephone **precall** (using either a calling list of known telephone numbers or RDD). Advance letters are also called "preletters." Introductory telephone calls describe and schedule an interview rather than administer it.

By reducing the surprise element and increasing the time that a potential respondent has to think about participating in the survey, advance letters and precalls can reduce refusal rates and increase data quality. These tools can also demonstrate the authenticity of the research so that the respondent does not assume that a sales pitch is coming.

Use of the following guidelines can help ensure that the introductory letter makes an appropriate impression on the respondent.

Guidelines for Preparing Advance Letters

- Use letterhead.
- For manageable sample sizes, use a personal salutation (e.g., Dear Mr. Jones), sign each letter individually in ink, and address each envelope individually rather than using labels.
- Date the letter to coincide with the mailing. A nondated letter gives it a less personal intrepretation.
- Provide an introductory statement regarding a future call or visit to conduct an interview, including timing of the contact, how the respondent was sampled and chosen, and whether someone else in the household might be ultimately interviewed.

- Describe the survey topic without being intimidating.
- Guarantee whatever level of confidentiality is possible.
- Give an honest estimate of the time required to complete the interview.
- Convey the importance of respondent views for valid results and potential impact.

It is important to convey an impression of legitimacy by having appropriate identification of the sponsor and source of the survey. Printed letterhead helps provide this identification. It is also crucial that respondents receive as personal an appeal as possible. They should feel that they were singled out for this interview and that *their* opinion is crucial to the study. Personalization through individualized salutations, original (not "rubber stamp") signatures, and individually typed envelopes have been shown to stimulate response, particularly from somewhat reluctant respondents (Frey, 1989). Of course, personalization is expensive to implement and cannot always be done for very large samples.

Information about the timing of a future contact helps respondents anticipate the call or visit and provides an opportunity to consider whether to participate in the survey. As with introductory statements in general, other details about sampling, survey topic, confidentiality, and so forth give respondents the necessary information on which to base their decision.

Advance letters may come directly from the survey group (see Examples 2.3 and 2.4) or may be an endorsement from a supporter or collaborator whom the person trusts (Example 2.5).

EXAMPLE 2.3
Advance Letter: Telephone Interview

(LETTERHEAD - CENTER FOR SURVEY RESEARCH)

Date

Mr. Bill Jones
2222 Elm Street
Las Vegas, NV 89000

Dear Mr. Jones:

During the week of June 3-10 an interviewer from the Center for Survey Research at the University of Nevada, Las Vegas, will be calling your home in connection with a survey of Clark County residents for their views on important community issues, such as transportation, growth, education, and the Yucca Mountain repository site.

Your name and number were selected at random from the local telephone directory. We are writing this letter because many people prefer to be informed in advance that a request for interview will be made in the near future. When the interviewer calls, he or she will request to speak to an adult, either you or another adult over the age of 18, in the household. This is done in order to be certain that all Clark County opinions are represented in the survey.

The interview should take approximately 10 minutes. Naturally, all of the responses will be confidential, and you can end the interview at any time.

Your participation will be greatly appreciated. This is a very important study for Clark County, and the results will be used by county officials in the formulating of policy for the area. If you have any questions, please feel free to call me at 555-1234. Thank you.

Sincerely,

James H. Frey, Ph.D.
Project Director

This advance letter is sent directly from the survey center using its letterhead.

EXAMPLE 2.4
Advance Letter: In-Home Interview

(LETTERHEAD - CENTER FOR SURVEY RESEARCH)

Date

Mr. Bill Jones
2222 Elm Street
Las Vegas, NV   89000

Dear Mr. Jones:

Recently you were called by the Center for Survey Research from the University of Nevada, Las Vegas, about participating in an extremely important study regarding issues facing the Clark County area (e.g., transportation, public safety, economic growth, and repository site). We need your opinions so we may help the county and the state prepare for the future. Your participation and cooperation are important so that the results of the research can be statistically valid. Please understand that you are one of 755 persons who have been scientifically selected from all adult residents of the Clark County urban area. Your responses will be treated with complete confidentiality.

We understand that you may have doubts about many appeals you receive for your opinion, particularly if that request is by telephone. We are not attempting to sell you anything; we only want your opinions. If you wish to verify this, or if you have any questions about the intent or purpose of this study, you can call me directly at the Center for Survey Research. The number is 555-1234.

When our interviewer calls you within the next few days, we would appreciate your making an appointment for an interview. We would like to conduct this interview in your home, and it will last approximately 45 minutes. Thank you for your consideration.

Sincerely,

James H. Frey, Ph.D.
Project Director
Center for Survey Research

P.S. We obtained your telephone number and address from the
    Hill-Donnelly Criss-Cross Directory, which matches listed
    telephone numbers and addresses.

This advance letter is sent from the survey center on its letterhead to inform a potential respondent that a request for an in-person interview is going to be made by telephone.

EXAMPLE 2.5
Advance Letter From a Trusted Collaborator
(PHYSICIAN'S LETTERHEAD)

Dear Ms. Smith:

I have been asked by the University of California to help them in a national study about the overall health of Americans. Many individuals from all parts of the country are being invited to help in this study.

In order to get correct information about the health of Americans I need your cooperation. Because this study is important I am asking my patients to take part in it. You can help me by answering a number of questions about your health. A study staff member will come to your home, or some other place if you prefer, to ask you some questions. The interview should take about an hour of your time.

The information you give will be kept strictly confidential. When your interview is finished, your name will be removed from the questionnaire. The answers you give will be combined with the answers given by all other persons interviewed and used for scientific study.

Please drop the enclosed postcard in the mail so that a member of the study staff may call you and answer any questions you may have and also arrange the best time and place for your interview. Or, if you prefer, the project staff or I would be glad to answer any questions. The staff can be reached at (310) 555-1234 (CALL COLLECT IF THIS IS OUT OF YOUR AREA).

I urge you to participate in this important study by the University of California conducted under the sponsorship of the National Institutes of Health.

Sincerely,

James Jones, M.D.

When confidentiality is of great concern, as in the case of having chosen a respondent from a medical records review in which sensitive information may be involved, the advance letter might come from a physician the respondent knows and trusts. If the physician is part of the survey team or clearly endorses the project, the letter serves to legitimize the study and make the respondent less uncomfortable about revealing personal information.

Similar to advance letters, precalls serve to inform respondents of their selection for interview and should include the same basic information about the survey. A future phone call (or visit) for an interview can be scheduled if the person consents. The precall can be referred to in the opening comments when the actual interview is done.

Advance letters, precalls, and introductory statements made immediately before the interview is administered all serve to entice the respondent into participating. One must be certain, however, that an *eligible* respondent has actually been contacted before the interview should proceed.

Eligibility Screen

In the course of the survey introduction it is important to determine whether the respondent is actually eligible to answer the questions. This is accomplished using an **eligibility screen.** In surveys of the general public, one is often interested in polling the views of individuals with specific characteristics, such as being registered voters or the person who most often does the grocery shopping for the family. If the survey respondents are grouped on a sampling list that was generated according to inclusion criteria (e.g., mothers of children with speech impairments who have received speech therapy at a local clinic), one presumably knows the name of the desired respondent and can ask for that person directly. This does not necessarily ensure eligibility, however, because there may be other criteria that need to be reviewed with the respondent directly (e.g., you may only be interested in mothers who also have at least one other child in the household). Interviewers must be trained in the importance of eligibility criteria and cautioned not to accept convenient substitutes.

The eligibility screen consists of one or more questions designed to determine whether the potential respondent has the characteristics the surveyor considers important. These questions should be asked after rapport has been established during the introductory phase and before the interview begins. Truthful answers to eligibility questions are more likely because the respondent trusts that the interviewer's purpose is legitimate, and resources are not wasted interviewing ineligible respondents whose data will have to be disregarded.

Example 2.6 illustrates both telephone and in-person eligibility screens.

EXAMPLE 2.6
Eligibility Screens

Telephone

1. Hello, my name is _____. I'm calling on behalf of Global Life Insurance Plan. We are speaking to persons who recently chose to terminate Global coverage to learn why they made that decision. Did you choose to leave Global, or did you have to leave because you were covered through your employer and you changed jobs or lost your job? (IF RESPONDENT CHOSE TO LEAVE, CONTINUE WITH INTERVIEW. IF RESPONDENT DID NOT CHOOSE TO LEAVE, THANK AND TERMINATE INTERVIEW.) Can I have a few minutes of your time to ask some questions about your opinions of Global? I can assure you that the information you give me will be confidential. It will be combined with information from several hundred other people and reported in statistical form only.

2. Good morning/evening. My name is _____ , and I'm calling from the Center for Survey Research at the University of Nevada, Las Vegas. We are conducting a survey of area residents on health issues. Today we are asking community residents 18 to 54 years old what they know about AIDS. Are you in this age group? (IF YES, CONTINUE. IF NO, ASK TO SPEAK TO SOMEONE ELSE IN THE HOUSEHOLD WHO IS THE SPECIFIED AGE. IF NO ONE IS AVAILABLE, THANK THEM FOR THEIR TIME AND TERMINATE THE INTERVIEW.) To assure you that your identity and responses will remain confidential, I want you to know that your telephone number was generated by a computer. I do not know your name or address, and I will not ask you for them. May I please have a few minutes of your time for this important survey? Thank you.

In Person

Hi. I'm with the Southern California Beaches Health Survey. We are here at the beach today asking families about their contact with the water. In about 10 days, another person from the survey or I will phone those who talk to us today. We will ask some follow-up questions about the water. We will also ask some health questions at that time. Are you willing to answer some questions today? Are you here with your family? (IF YES, PROCEED WITH SCREENING QUESTIONS.)

1. Have you or anyone in your household been swimming or playing in the water at this beach today?

      Yes   →   CONTINUE TO Q2
      No   →   THANK AND END INTERVIEW

2. Not including (3-day survey period), do you think you or anyone in your household will return to this beach in the next 10 days?

Yes, we will all return   →   THANK AND END INTERVIEW

Yes, some of us will return   →   CONTINUE **ONLY** FOR THOSE WHO WILL **NOT** RETURN BUT WHO **HAVE BEEN IN THE WATER**

No, none of us will return   →   CONTINUE INTERVIEW FOR ENTIRE HOUSEHOLD

SOURCE: Adapted from the *Santa Monica Beach Study Pilot*.

These examples are introductory scripts containing eligibility screens specific to the needs of the particular survey. In the first example, a respondent is eligible only if termination of insurance coverage was voluntary because the surveyor wants to know the reasons why people chose to discontinue coverage. In the second example, the respondents are eligible only if they fall into a specific age group in whose opinions the surveyor is interested. In the third example, which is a face-to-face encounter, the surveyor wants to limit findings to a single day of contact with the water during a specified period of time. Thus, anyone who may come back to the beach during that period is not eligible.

Often, it is necessary to sample within a household or living unit, particularly if an individual, not a household, is the unit of analysis. Because households can be clusters of eligible respondents, it is necessary to sample within the cluster to obtain a random probability sample. In some cases, it is only necessary to get responses from any member of the household who is familiar with the survey topic. It is also not necessary to implement a within-household selection procedure if the eligibility screen is directed at a very specific member, say, a female over the age of 55 or a member of the household who plays golf or has a disability. If such criteria are not defined, then one of several selection procedures is used. We discuss these only briefly here (for a more exhaustive review, see Dillman, 1978; Frey, 1989).

The selection of the *first eligible* respondent to come to the telephone or answer the door is often implemented when resources are limited and time may be a factor. In this case, the surveyor verifies that the potential respondent meets minimum qualification criteria (e.g., "Over the age of 18" or "Lived in household for more than 3 months" and then conducts the interview. This selection process produces a "convenience" sample that is not a probability design. Generalization to the larger population can be made only with some caution. This technique oversamples females, particularly in telephone surveys where women tend to answer the phone in a household. Some researchers implement a *male-female alternate* selection process, but this assumes that the distribution of gender is known and that substitution does not compromise the distribution of population characteristics.

Another type of selection procedure calls for the *enumeration of household members.* This technique asks for a listing of all members of a household by age, gender, and relation to head of household, and a respondent is then chosen from among them. This technique is time consuming and more demanding of interviewers. It produces higher-than-normal refusal rates because many households are headed by women who resist describing the composition of their home to strangers. This technique is more successful with in-person interviews than with those conducted by telephone.

One technique that is gaining in popularity with surveyors asks for the person in the household who has had the *last birthday* or will have the *next birthday*. The request for birthday information is not threatening to the respondent, and the probability of selection is preserved because it is assumed that the distribution of birthdays in a population is random, not systematic or patterned in any way. The interviewer simply asks,

> "We need to be sure we give every adult a chance to be interviewed for this study. Thinking only of adults in your household, that is, persons over the age of 18, which one had the most recent birthday? (or will have the next birthday)? Would you be that person?"
>
> IF YES, CONTINUE INTERVIEW
> IF NO, "May I speak to that person?"
> (REPEAT INTRODUCTION)

Very often, the person answering the telephone or initially responding to an in-person interview request is also the eligible respondent, that is, has the next or most recent birthday. In practice, the use of "last birthday" is preferable to using "next birthday" because it is easier to recall who had a birthday than to remember who will have one in the future.

Questions From Respondents

At some time during the introduction and the eligibility screen, potential respondents or other family members are very likely to ask questions regarding the survey to determine whether it is legitimate and to help them decide whether or not to participate. Although some of these questions might come up at the end of the interview or even during its administration, most will be asked near the beginning of the contact. Such questions must be answered in a consistent manner by all interviewers, with interviewers trained not to add information that could bias a respondent's answers. The questions most likely to be asked by respondents should have standardized responses (sometimes called "fallback statements") developed and made available to the interviewers.

Interviewers need to be very familiar with these standardized responses and keep them readily available as a memory backup during the interview. They should be instructed to call on a supervisor to respond to questions they cannot answer. In the case of telephone interviews done in a survey center, supervisors are immediately available to answer the question. However, in both small-scale phone interviews done from interviewers' homes and in-person interviews, no supervisors are present, so interviewers should tell respondents that a supervisor will call them soon to answer their questions (remember to write down the telephone number).

Some of the questions frequently asked by respondents are the following:

> "How did you get my name (telephone number, address)?"
> "Whom do you represent?"
> "Who is sponsoring this survey?"
> "Will you use my name?"
> "How will you use my answers?"
> "Will this cost me anything, or will I be paid for my participation?"
> "What will happen if I don't participate?"

A few other questions will probably come to mind related to the specific survey being conducted (e.g., in a survey of satisfaction with health care, respondents might want to know whether their doctor will have access to their responses or name).

Example 2.7 lists possible questions that respondents might have regarding a nuclear power survey and the prepared answers supplied to interviewers.

EXAMPLE 2.7
Standardized Responses to Respondent
Questions About a Nuclear Power Survey

What is the Center for Survey Research?

This is a research unit of the University of Nevada, Las Vegas, designed for the purpose of conducting public opinion polls and surveys on various social, political, and economic issues. The director is Dr. James Frey, also a member of the Sociology Department. If you have any questions or concerns about participating in this study, you can contact him at 555-1234.

Who is paying for this research?

This is a cooperative project funded by the Sagebrush Alliance and the Department of Sociology at UNLV.

Who or what is the Sagebrush Alliance?

The Sagebrush Alliance is a community group concerned with the evaluation of the impact of environmental changes on the quality of life of residents of the state of Nevada.

How did you get my name?

We do not have or need your name. Your number was dialed at random using a technique called random digit dialing. We did not use a list, such as the telephone directory, to get your name.

How do I know that this is confidential?

We do not have your name. We are interested only in combining the responses of the 400 or so persons who will be called. Individual responses will not be singled out. All of us working on this project are required to follow certain procedures and guidelines developed to protect the identity of persons who respond to the survey.

How will the results be used?

The information generated by this survey will be used by students in research methods classes. The results will also be made available to policymakers in the community to help them know and understand what county residents think about the nature and use of nuclear energy and about other issues.

What is the purpose of the survey?

This is a general survey of the public on a number of community issues including nuclear power. The study is designed to learn more about the public's opinions and perceptions.

How long will this take?

The interview should take about 10 minutes. You can end the interview at any time, but we hope you will not.

WARNING

 Do not provide any additional information to the standardized responses. If there are questions that you cannot answer or if your answer does not satisfy the respondent, call the supervisor.

Dealing with questions about conditions and intent of the survey is an important part of interviewer training, especially for field interviewers who cannot be monitored closely. Telephone interviewers in a centralized location can be easily monitored for responses, and corrections can be made immediately, if necessary.

Interview Questions

Once eligible respondents have agreed to participate, the real substance of the interview, the questioning, can begin. The design of questions for interviews is a complex process involving many considerations. The basic task is twofold: Write the questions and organize them into a coherent document, the questionnaire. The goals of question writing are to encompass content relevant to the survey objectives, use language that is meaningful to the target group, and use a presentation style that maximizes valid and reliable responses. The goals of questionnaire organization are to create smooth conversational flow for both the respondent and the interviewer and to provide structure for those who prepare the data for analysis—the coder who translates the answers into numeric codes and the data-entry person who enters the codes into a computer for analysis (for more information regarding coding and data entry, see **How to Analyze Survey Data**, Vol. 8 in this series).

CONTENT

The primary purpose of the questions is to meet the objectives of the survey. Deciding on the content of survey questions requires operationalizing the problems the survey is expected to address. This can be done by listing topic areas, or variables, that must be covered in an interview and/or ideas about the relationships among variables. Once these variables have been defined, decisions can be made about how they will be measured. The basic steps are listed in the following checklist.

Checklist for Determining Question Content

✓ **List the survey objectives.**

✓ **Conceptualize the components of each objective by listing relevant topics.**

✓ **Frame questions for each topic.**

Example 2.8 illustrates how the surveyor goes about capturing the survey objectives in the questions.

EXAMPLE 2.8
Operationalizing the Survey Problem

A survey has the following objective: To assess satisfaction among participants of a perinatal outreach program for low-income women in Los Angeles County.

The surveyor first operationalizes satisfaction by listing relevant topics:

1. Levels of satisfaction with specific program services

2. Reasons for dissatisfaction with program services

3. Perceived impact of program services on quality of life

4. Suggestions for program improvement

Then the questions are developed to measure satisfaction:

1. The first question set asks about satisfaction with each program service (referrals to prenatal care, transportation to prenatal visits, baby-sitting during prenatal visits, and housing assistance) is developed. The respondent is asked if she needed each service, and if so, whether the service was provided by the program. If yes, she is asked how satisfied she was with the service, using a scale from extremely satisfied to extremely dissatisfied.

2. The next set of questions refers the respondent back to every service with which she said she was dissatisfied. She is then asked why she was dissatisfied. No response options are offered because the surveyor does not want to influence what might be said. Possible responses are anticipated, however, and listed for easy check-off by the interviewer. Space for unanticipated responses is also provided.

3. Because the surveyor conceptualizes satisfaction to include a sense that quality of life has been improved by program participation, a third set of questions is developed asking whether program participation improved the respondent's quality of life. For purposes of this survey, quality of life is defined as: lowered daily stress level, improved sense of overall well-being, improved sense of personal health, and increased expectation of a healthy delivery. The respondent is asked to what degree program participation improved her quality of life in each area (very much to not at all).

4. The questionnaire ends with an open-ended question (one without possible answers for the respondent to choose from) asking for suggestions for program improvement.

Items for a survey may be written entirely from scratch, or items shown to collect valid data may be borrowed from other surveys. For example, the surveyor in Example 2.8 may postulate (form a hypothesis) that there is a relationship between depression levels among respondents and satisfaction with services. Depression may be common in this population of socially disadvantaged women. It may be a barrier to meaningful program participation and thus cause a respondent to be more likely to be dissatisfied. A known depression scale could be found in the literature and used in the survey to distinguish "depressed" from "nondepressed" respondents. (Some wording of items might need to be adapted to the target population.) In the analysis, the satisfaction level of depressed versus nondepressed respondents could be compared to see if there is a difference. If there is, a program modification could be planned to address this need, perhaps by adding social workers or psychologists to the outreach team.

To write the questions described in Example 2.8, the surveyor must take into account the characteristics, such as age and education level, of the respondents. In the example, respondents are to be asked whether program participation improved their overall sense of well-being. The women in the target group have low incomes, low expected levels of education, and possibly poor English-language skills because of the large Hispanic population in Los Angeles County. A question such as "How much did participation in this program improve your overall sense of well-being?" might not be very meaningful to these respondents. A more appropriate question might read as follows:

> "Since this program has been helping you, have you been feeling better in your everyday life?"
> IF YES, "Would you say you are feeling a lot, some, or a little better than before you found the program?"

Putting the question into simpler language better communicates the intent of the surveyor and is more consistent with the education and language-skill levels of the population.

WORDING

Wording questions is not as simple a task as it might seem. Stanley Payne (1951), in his classic book *The Art of Asking Questions*, enumerates 100 different factors that affect the form and content of each question appearing on the survey questionnaire. The survey problem and its theoretical or practical rationale, of course, should be the prominent factor in determining the questions that will be asked and the form that each question will take. Each question represents an "operationalization" of some component of the survey problem and a measurement, or quantifiable assessment, of that component. Thus, the question must be structured in a neutral fashion so that the respondent is not predisposed to a certain answer pattern. It must be justifiable in terms of its relation to previous and subsequent questions.

All questions must mean the same to both the respondent and the surveyor (Frey, 1989). This is a difficult task to accomplish.

The use of a **questionnaire map,** or explicit review of the justification for each question, which is covered in interviewer training, helps the interviewer understand the question and consequently communicate properly with the respondent. Pretests will help determine if respondents generally understand the question. There are several criteria to apply when selecting questions and their subsequent wording:

- The topic of each question is relevant to the research goal.
- The comprehensibility of the question has been established at a level consistent with the characteristics of the population.

- The question is consistent with previous and subsequent questions. Transition facilitates this connection.
- The question phrasing is neutral.
- The question pertains to only one concept or issue.
- The question is considered a valid measure of the concept of interest.
- Questions produce a minimum of nonsubstantive responses (e.g., "Don't Know" or "No Answer").
- Response categories on closed items are exhaustive and mutually exclusive.
- Pretest responses to the question produce sufficient variation rather than finding all responses in one category, such as "None."
- Interviewers experience no difficulty administering the question.
- Respondents do not have to ask the interviewer to rephrase or repeat the question.
- Coders have no difficulty coding responses for data entry.

There are many excellent discussions of question wording—for example, Payne (1951), Dillman (1978), Oppenheim (1992), and Schuman and Presser (1981). Specific guidelines for formulating survey objectives and determining variables of interest together with the mechanics of question wording, question types, formatting, and use of scales are described in **How to Ask Survey Questions** (Vol. 2 in this series).

Knowledge and behavior questions are the easiest to write because they generally are straightforward. "How often have you attended religious services or events in the past month?" and "Have you heard about the proposal to locate a nuclear waste repository at Yucca Mountain?" are examples. Often, they serve as filter questions, where one response (e.g., not heard of repository) leads to a sequence of questions that is different from the sequence asked of those who have heard of the repository.

The most difficult questions to ask concern attitude; they present the greatest problems with reliability and validity because of their focus on subjective dimensions (e.g., attitudes, beliefs, values, and opinions). Attitude items are indirect measures of these factors and therefore more difficult to construct because these dimensions vary in intensity, primacy, importance, and concern to respondents. Sometimes, respondents' difficulty understanding such questions can be lessened using visual aids, but this is, of course, possible only with in-person surveys.

Guidelines for Question Wording

- Avoid "loaded" questions that suggest to the respondent that one answer is preferable to another.

- Avoid the use of inflammatory words, such as "communist," "racist," or "exploitation."

- Be natural in wording but not folksy. Questions should have a conversational tone, written in much the same way as people talk.

- Avoid the use of slang terms or colloquialisms that may be understood by only a small subset of the population.

- Avoid the use of technical terms or abbreviations that might be misinterpreted. Not everyone knows that AMA stands for the American Medical Association.

- Be specific in the use of terms and concepts (e.g., government —which level? Federal, state, or local?).

- Be specific when using a time period as a referent for recall or a time limit on behavior.

- Make sure that facts contained within the question are accurate. Nothing can make an interviewer look more foolish than to present incorrect information, particularly to a knowledgeable respondent.
- Be careful not to *assume behavior* or *assume knowledge* on the part of the respondent.
- Use correct grammar and sentence structure (e.g., verb tense, no double negatives).
- Avoid double questions where two or more issues are mentioned. Split the question. It is difficult to determine the meaning of a response to a question like "Are you satisfied with the university and the Sociology Department?"
- Response categories should match the dimension addressed in the question. For example, do not list "Yes" and "No" as response categories when you ask for the extent to which respondents agree or disagree.
- Response categories should be mutually exclusive, thus limiting the respondent to one alternative.
- Ask questions about past or present behavior rather than about future behavior. A person's predictions of future behavior are very unreliable.
- Avoid all-inclusive terms, such as "never" or "always."
- Questions should include the response categories of "Don't Know" or "Refuse to Answer," but these are only read to the respondent when appropriate.
- Clearly communicate to respondents just how they are to answer the question. That is, make sure they know how to answer by reading the response in the context of the question. For example, "Do you strongly agree, agree, disagree, or strongly disagree that the benefits of the nuclear repository will outweigh the costs?"
- Avoid list that includes more than five items. Respondents will not be able to recall the list unless it is provided in the form of a visual aid.

- Be as concrete, specific, and simple as possible in phrasing and wording. Write questions for the respondent, not you. Never assume that a respondent is anywhere near as familiar with a topic as you are.
- Prepare a list of neutral probes that interviewers may use with open-ended questions.

Although the questions that are asked in the course of a survey are mainly a function of the survey topic, the interview mode should also be considered in deciding what can be asked and how the questions should be worded. The interview mode plays a major role in determining questioning styles.

Styles of Questioning

The in-person interview makes possible a wide range of questioning styles because of the greater opportunity to probe, to read nonverbal cues, and to use visual aids. The telephone interview places some limitations on question wording because of the inability to use visual cues to assist the respondent in retaining the contents of lengthy and/or complex questions. Respondents must understand questions and choose responses or rank items based on what can be kept in memory after the information is conveyed verbally by the interviewer. The respondent may not be able to remember all details of the question to voice an accurate opinion or may forget the first response option by the time the fourth is read. Also, the telephone interviewer has no ability to use facial expression or body language feedback to determine whether the respondent is following and comprehending and whether the pace of the questioning is appropriate. The overall goal to keep in mind when constructing questions for a telephone interview is to decrease complexity without compromising the depth and detail of the data to the point of meaninglessness.

Whenever possible, it is best to keep questions and response lists short and simple for both kinds of interviews. However, if a complex question is simplified too much, it may generate a large number of "no opinion" responses because the respondent doesn't have enough information to formulate an opinion. Detailed background information may be necessary prior to asking the question. Limiting response categories can be a problem if the options provided do not provide the detail needed for meaningfulness. The in-person interview can deal with these problems by using visual aids. In Example 2.9, lists of response options matching those that the interviewer sees on the questionnaire are handed to the respondent for reference when answering the question.

EXAMPLE 2.9
Visual Aids

Complex Response Options

QUESTION

31. Regarding **physical** activity, compared to others of your age and sex, when you were *(read age group below)*, were you *(read choices)*?

(Show Flashcard H)

	Much Less Active	Less Active	Average	More Active	Much More Active
Teens and early 20's	1	2	3	4	5
Late 20's and 30's	1	2	3	4	5
40's	1	2	3	4	5
50's	1	2	3	4	5
60's	1	2	3	4	5
70's	1	3	3	4	5

FLASHCARD H

	MUCH LESS ACTIVE	LESS ACTIVE	AVERAGE	MORE ACTIVE	MUCH MORE ACTIVE
TEENS AND EARLY 20'S	1	2	3	4	5
LATE 20'S AND 30'S	1	2	3	4	5
40'S	1	2	3	4	5
50'S	1	2	3	4	5
60'S	1	2	3	4	5
70'S	1	2	3	4	5

SOURCE: From the Kaiser/UCLA Sigmoid Study.

This flashcard allows the respondent to study the list of complex response options without forgetting any of the choices in determining the answer for each relevant age.

75

Long List of Complex Responses

QUESTION

What is your natural adult hair color?

(Show Flashcard I)

Bright red	1
Red	2
Light blonde	3
Blonde (whole life)	4
Light brown (blonde as child)	5
Light brown (whole life)	6
Medium brown	7
Auburn (dark red-brown)	8
Dark brown/black	9
Jet black	10

FLASHCARD I

BRIGHT RED

RED

LIGHT BLONDE

BLONDE (WHOLE LIFE)

LIGHT BROWN
(BLONDE AS CHILD)

LIGHT BROWN (WHOLE LIFE)

MEDIUM BROWN

AUBURN (DARK RED-BROWN)

DARK BROWN/BLACK

JET BLACK

SOURCE: From the Kaiser/UCLA Sigmoid Study.

This list not only involves complexity (different shades of hair color at different times of life), it is also rather long. This list would be very difficult to retain in memory if given over the phone but can be reviewed at the respondent's own pace during in-person interviews using a visual aid.

Another way of dealing with complexity is to use a variety of question-writing techniques. The techniques usually involve some method of reducing the complexity either by separating the question into components or by summarizing key components. The question is thereby simplified, and the numbers of response categories required for an individual question are reduced. The telephone interview relies much more heavily on these techniques than does the in-person interview. Techniques discussed here are the split, the funnel, the inverted funnel, the keyword summary, and recall.

SPLIT QUESTION TECHNIQUE

This technique reduces the complexity of a question area. It is similar to what is called the "unfolding" technique. The first question is general; a person may be asked to choose an answer from a list of options. Then, depending on the response to the first question, a clarifying question is asked, as shown in Example 2.10.

EXAMPLE 2.10
Split Question Technique for
Numerous Response Categories

Version Possible With Visual Aid Showing Responses

1. What was the highest level you finished in your education?

6th grade or less	1
Grade school through 6th	2
Some high school	3
Completed high school	4
Some college	5
Completed college (associate degree)	6
Completed college (bachelor's degree)	7
Advanced degree	8

Version Possible for Use in a Telephone Interview

1. What was the highest level you finished in your education?

Grade school	1
High school	2
College	3

IF THE RESPONDENT ANSWERS "COLLEGE"

1a. What is the highest degree you received?

Associate degree	1
Bachelor's degree	2
Master's degree	3
Doctorate	4

The split question technique reduces the number of responses that have to be considered at one time by separating the question so that some responses apply to the first question and some to the second. In this example, instead of listing eight education levels, the question is split so that respondents must only report their highest generic level of education for the first question. If the response is "college," a second question is asked to determine what level of college was completed.

The split question technique can also be used for ranking items. Ranking means putting items in order according to a criterion—for example, most important to least important. In the in-person interview, ranking is easily accomplished by handing the respondent a list of the items to be ranked, as in Example 2.11, or a set of cards showing one item on each card, which can simply be placed in rank order.

EXAMPLE 2.11
Visual Aid to List Response Options
for Priority Choice

QUESTION

Now, thinking about the chance of property damage, injuries, public health problems, and the loss of life, please rank the following hazards in order from most to least threatening to your community today.

HAND CARD TO RESPONDENT.
RECORD RANK ORDER IN RIGHT COLUMN.

Hazard	Ranking
Tornadoes	
Floods	
Earthquakes	
Water pollution	
Nuclear/radiation accident	
Hazardous chemical spill	
Don't know	

SOURCE: From the Kaiser/UCLA Sigmoid Study.

VISUAL AID

RESPONSE CARD

HAZARDS

Tornadoes
Floods
Earthquakes
Water Pollution
Nuclear/Radiation Accident
Hazardous Chemical Spill

Using this visual aid, respondents simply name the responses in the order they consider to be most to least threatening. The interviewer writes the ranking in the appropriate box on the interview form; the first hazard named is ranked 1, the second 2, and so on.

Without a visual aid, ranking is very difficult. However, the split technique reduces the difficulty. The respondent is read each item and asked for a general rating of priority or importance (e.g., very important, somewhat important, not important). The next question asks the respondent to state which item on the list is *most* important, which is second, and which is third, as illustrated in Example 2.12.

EXAMPLE 2.12
Split Question for Ranking

5. When choosing day care for their children, parents consider certain criteria in making a decision. Would you say each of the following criteria is very important, somewhat important, or not important to your own choice of day care for your children?

	Very Important	Somewhat Important	Not Important
Facility location	1	2	3
Cost	1	2	3
Staff training in child development	1	2	3
Hours of operation	1	2	3
Child/caregiver ratio	1	2	3
Lunch program	1	2	3

   5a. Of the criteria listed (READ THEM AGAIN), which is the most important to you?

_____

   5b. Which is the second most important?

_____

   5c. Which is the third most important?

_____

Although not all items are ranked in order with this technique, a sense of the general importance of each item is achieved using a 3-point scale (very important to not important). Then, the top three items are ranked in order, telling the surveyor what is most important to the respondent.

FUNNEL TECHNIQUE

This technique guides the respondent through a complex concept using a series of questions that progressively narrows the field of interest. The series progresses from the general to the specific and usually begins with an open-ended question (one without response options), followed by several closed-ended or forced-choice items (items that provide a list of answers to choose from), as shown in Example 2.13.

EXAMPLE 2.13
Funnel Technique

7. What criteria do you think the media should use in determining what should be made public about the personal lives of political candidates?

_____

_____

_____

7a. If the media suspects that a political candidate has committed a crime, when do you believe the information should be revealed to the public? (READ OPTIONS)

Immediately	1
Not until some evidence has been uncovered	2
Not unless the person is actually proven guilty	3

7b. How much of a candidate's personal life do you believe the public has a right to know about? Would you say (READ OPTIONS):

Everything is relevant to the candidate's character
and should therefore be known   1
Limited information relevant to the person's
policies (such as family life, military experience,
education) should be revealed   2
The person's personal life is private and should
not be publicized   3

The first question allows respondents to introduce any concepts, some of which the surveyor may not have anticipated. Now that the respondents are thinking in the right context, Questions 7a and 7b focus them on specific aspects that the surveyor has chosen to emphasize.

INVERTED FUNNEL TECHNIQUE

When a respondent is not expected to be knowledgeable about a content area or have an articulated opinion on a topic, the funnel technique may be reversed. Specific questions on components of the larger issue that one is interested in studying are asked first to focus and educate the respondent. The general question follows. Example 2.14 illustrates this technique.

EXAMPLE 2.14
Inverted Funnel Technique

1. Over the past years, how often would you say you have gambled for money?

> Not at all
> 1 - 3 times
> 4 - 6 times
> More than 6 times
> No answer

2. What versions of gambling are legal in your community?

Nothing is legal
Specify: _____

3. What is your view of the expanding legalization of many forms of gambling in America today?

_____

_____

_____

This series begins with specific questions to focus the respondent on gambling and then asks a broad question about expanding the legalization of gambling.

KEYWORD SUMMARY

After reading the background information that precedes a question on a complex issue, keywords can be summarized in a brief repeat statement, followed by the question itself. For example, respondents might not be able to render an opinion regarding a proposed new law without first hearing a detailed description of the law and its enforcement. A description of the law (using unbiased terms) followed by a keyword summary can help respondents grasp the issues well enough to state an opinion when subsequently asked "Would you be in favor of the passage of such a law?" Example 2.15 shows how this technique is used to gather respondents' views on a proposed nuclear waste repository.

EXAMPLE 2.15
Keyword Summary

The federal government is making plans to locate a high-level nuclear waste repository on Yucca Mountain, 120 miles northwest of Las Vegas. This waste would be stored in cast-iron containers 1,500 feet below ground, and the repository would be filled within 30 years, at which time the site would be sealed.

Some people in the state of Nevada think that Nevadans should stop fighting the repository and try, instead, to make a deal with the federal government to get as many benefits (e.g., cash for roads, tax rebates) as possible for the state if the site is located there. Others believe that Yucca Mountain is a poor choice and that the waste cannot be stored safely. Thus, the state should continue to resist locating the repository and not compromise its position by making a deal for benefits.

Keyword Summary

OK. Some people support the location of a repository in Nevada in order to get benefits from the federal government; others say it is not safe and the state should continue to resist.

How do you feel? Should the state stop its opposition and make a deal, or should the state continue to resist even if it means the loss of benefits?

> Stop resisting and make a deal
> Continue opposition to repository
> Don't know
> No answer

The detailed background information is necessary because not all respondents will have heard all relevant information through the media. It is too much, however, to keep in mind long enough to answer questions thoughtfully. The keyword summary reminds respondents of the key points to consider when answering the question.

RECALL TECHNIQUES

Special techniques to enhance response accuracy are used when designing questions requiring recall. Two of these are aided recall and bounded recall. The use of visual aids is also discussed.

Aided Recall

The problem of *omission*, or forgetting an event entirely, can be addressed using a form of **aided recall.** For example, recall can be stimulated by presenting a list of events or behaviors and asking if the respondent has taken part. Instead of asking the open-ended question "What leisure activities have you participated in during the past year?", a list of activities is presented, and the respondent is asked to choose all that apply. For a telephone interview, the lists must be short, although several sets can be presented separately. This is not a problem in the in-person interview because lists can simply be handed to the respondent for review to make sure nothing is omitted.

Another technique is to ask respondents to recall a reference point and then guide them through time. One might ask respondents to recall a major event, such as a first job. A career progression across time could then be reconstructed with reference to the first job. Example 2.16 shows how aided recall using a reference point is applied to a question on weight.

EXAMPLE 2.16
Aided Recall Using a Reference Point: Weight at 18 Years of Age

63. Approximately how much did you weigh when you were 18 years old?

_____ pounds

RECORD THIS WEIGHT IN COLUMN B OF AGE/WEIGHT CHART

Prompt: **This is around the age people graduate from high school.**

64a. Until what age did you continue to weigh between
(plus or minus 10 pounds of the last weight given)?

RECORD THE AGE AT WHICH RESPONDENT'S
WEIGHT CHANGED ON THE NEXT LINE, COLUMN
A, OF THE AGE/WEIGHT CHART. IF RESPONDENT IS
UNABLE TO GIVE ACCURATE INFORMATION IN
10-POUND INTERVALS, ACCEPT RESPONDENT'S
BEST ESTIMATE.

64b. How much did you weigh when you were
(age last entered in the chart)?

CONTINUE TO ASK Q64 UNTIL YOU HAVE
REACHED RESPONDENT'S CURRENT AGE AND
WEIGHT. IF RESPONDENT IS A FEMALE, DO *NOT*
RECORD WEIGHT CHANGES DUE TO PREGNANCY
BUT DO RECORD A WEIGHT CHANGE THAT IS
MAINTAINED 6 MONTHS AFTER DELIVERY.

65. **AGE/WEIGHT CHART**

	A	B
	AGE	**WEIGHT**
1.	18	
2.		
3.		
4.		
5.		
6.		
7.		
8.		
9.		
10.		

Another problem of recall questions, **telescoping,** or the tendency to report an event as having taken place more recently than it actually did, can be lessened if responses can be verified with a record. For example, a respondent might consult a weekly planner to verify the actual date of the last homeowner's association meeting attended. Depending on the record required, this can be very hard to do over the telephone, although a letter sent in advance could instruct the respondent to have a particular record available at the time of the interview. During the in-person interview, the interviewer can wait while documents are located and can even help interpret them.

Another approach is to use **landmark events** as a reference. For example, a respondent could be asked if a behavior occurred before or after the last election. Holidays and celebrations, major disasters, noteworthy international events like the Olympics, and high-profile media publicity of events like the O. J. Simpson trial are examples of landmark occurrences that can serve as adequate time referents because they are generally known to everyone. The in-person interviewer can use a calendar or timeline showing landmark events to visually assist a respondent in reconstructing the timing of events.

Bounded Recall

If sufficient funds are available, a technique called **bounded recall** can be used. Here, two interviews are conducted where questions in the second interview are phrased in reference to the time elapsed since the first interview. That is, during the second interview the surveyor can ask the respondent about certain behaviors/activities (e.g., played golf, absent from work, went to church) that have taken place since the first interview was conducted. This technique is more feasibly used in telephone interviewing because reinterviewing each respondent in person is very costly. Bounded recall can be implemented if a panel study is being conducted and the surveyor wants to prevent what is known as "forward telescoping," or the tendency to include more and earlier events in the time frame specified by the interviewer (see Converse & Presser, 1986).

Visual Aids

The in-person interview can use all of the questioning techniques described in preceding sections, including the use of visual aids. Besides helping respondents cope with complex or long lists of response options and questions requiring recall, visual aids can also help respondents deal with scales that require estimations, as illustrated in Example 2.17.

EXAMPLE 2.17
Use of Visual Aid for Rating Scale
Requiring a Visual Estimate

QUESTION

I'm going to ask you how *you* feel about various government agencies and institutions. Please tell me how much you trust . . .

	NO TRUST										COMPLETE TRUST
The President	0	1	2	3	4	5	6	7	8	9	10

VISUAL AID

RATING SCALE—TRUST

NO TRUST										COMPLETE TRUST
0	1	2	3	4	5	6	7	8	9	10

Using this visual rating scale, respondents estimate the amount of their trust in the President by looking at the scale and specifying a point that corresponds to that amount.

The uses and types of visual aids are virtually limitless. Some of the more common ones (including those previously described) are the following:

- List of response options (if complex or numerous)
- List of items to aid recall
- Rating scale requiring a visual estimate
- Information summary relevant to forming opinions for a question or question sequence
- Lists of information to educate the respondent
- Lists from which to make priority choices
- Photographs (e.g., pictures of medications) to aid recall
- Cards containing one item each for ranking
- Calendars to aid recall of timing of events
- Maps to clarify geographic relationships

Many other kinds of visual aids may be developed. Their design is part of the task of question writing. The next task is the organization of those questions.

Organization and Format

Once the questions and any visual aids have been developed, they must be organized into a questionnaire. Organization refers not only to the order in which the questions are presented but also the instructional guidelines for the interviewer and coder that hold all of the parts of the questionnaire together. The task of organizing the interview questions should be guided by two primary criteria: "flow" of the questionnaire and the potential question order effects. The transition from question to question and from question group to question group needs to consider the expectations and tasks of the interviewer, the respondent, and the data-entry person. Minimizing the effect of question order on response patterns requires careful consideration of how a respondent's exposure to one question might influence how a subsequent question is answered.

The following guidelines are helpful in maintaining the conversational flow of the interview while also providing clarity and logic for the respondent and the coder. Smooth question sequencing makes both the respondent's and the interviewer's task easier; disorganized interviewing increases error from inaccurate responses and results in lower response rates.

Guidelines for Questionnaire Flow

- Use a smooth conversational tone in all portions of the interview that are read to the respondent. This includes instructions, probes, and prompts.

- Set up the page so that interviewer instructions and coding guidelines are clearly distinguishable from the portions to be read aloud to the respondent; this may be accomplished using different fonts, typefaces, and graphics, such as instruction boxes. One of the best ways to distinguish instructions from questions is to put the instructions to interviewers in CAPS.

- Use directions and arrows to guide the interviewer through the form.

- Avoid organizing items in a way that requires the interviewer to page back and forth in the questionnaire; if reference to previous information needs to be made, repeat it.

The questionnaire items shown in Example 2.18 illustrate interviewer instructions that enhance flow.

EXAMPLE 2.18
Instructions to Enhance Flow

1. FIRST, I'D LIKE TO START BY ASKING YOU SOME GENERAL QUESTIONS ABOUT YOURSLF.

   What is your date of birth?

   _____ / _____ / _____
   Month   Day   Year

(Compute current age here: _____ years; also *code age*
    on p. 27)*

2. What is your current marital status?

   Married 1
   Widowed . . . . 2 → SKIP TO Q4
   Separated or divorced . . . . 3 → SKIP TO Q4
   Never married . . . . 4 → SKIP TO Q4

3. Do you live with your wife/husband?

   Yes . . . . 1 → SKIP TO Q6
   No 2

4. Do you live alone?

   Yes . . . . 1 → SKIP TO Q6
   No 2

5. Do you live with other family members or with someone else?

   *(Circle only one; if respondent lives with other family members,
       circle 1 even if respondent **also** lives with someone else)*

   With other family members 1
   With someone else 2

6. NOW I WOULD LIKE TO LEARN MORE ABOUT MEMBERS
   OF YOUR FAMILY.

   *(Go to the SUPPLEMENT for the questions to use with this
       section)*

These instructions represent conventions to be used throughout
this particular survey to tell the interviewer how to proceed.

SOURCE: From the Kaiser/UCLA Sigmoid Study.

In this example, transition statements (statements that introduce and separate sections) are given in capital letters, instructions to the interviewer are in italics, and skip patterns are designated with arrows followed by the number of the question to which the interviewer should skip. Although these conventions apply only to this particular questionnaire, every interview questionnaire should adopt standardized conventions to keep the interviewer from getting lost on the page or reading something aloud that is not intended for the respondent.

All of the anticipated answers already have a code assigned (in Question 2, married is coded 1, widowed is coded 2, etc.), making the task of recording responses very straightforward: The number of the answer given is simply circled. The coder then has no problem transferring responses to the database because they are already coded. Any time that responses could be coded in a variety of ways (as for open-ended questions), standardized coding instructions to the interviewer should be printed on the form to make coding, and therefore data entry, as clear as possible. Example 2.19 illustrates other forms of interviewer instructions.

EXAMPLE 2.19
Interviewer Instructions

Transit Survey

Hello. This is _____ calling from the Center for Survey Research at the University of Nevada, Las Vegas. We are conducting an opinion survey of Clark County residents about public transportation in the area. Your phone number was selected at random, and we do not need your name and address. All of your responses will be confidential, and the questions

I need to ask will take only a few minutes. OK? Before we continue, I need to know if you are 17 years of age or older.

IF YES, ASK: "What is your age?" _____ years.
(CONTINUE INTERVIEW)

IF NO, ASK: "Is there anyone 17 years of age or older with whom we may talk?"

IF YES, REPEAT INTRODUCTION AND CONTINUE INTERVIEW.

IF NO, TERMINATE INTERVIEW: "Thank you. We need to talk with persons 17 years of age or older."

Baseline Survey for High-Level Nuclear Waste Repository Risks

INTRODUCTION: PART I

Hello, my name is _____. We're conducting a study of energy and the environmental issues. I'm calling from the JHF Corporation, a national survey research firm. As part of the study, I'd like to interview the male decision maker in the household over 18 years of age.

1. Would that be you?

Yes   1   → GO TO INTRODUCTION, PART II

No   2

↓

1a. May I speak with him now?

Yes   1   → REPEAT INTRODUCTION, PART I AND GO TO INTRODUCTION, PART II

No   2

INTRODUCTION: PART II

We're interested in learning your attitudes and opinions on issues about energy and the environment. You may choose not to answer a question or simply say "don't know" if that's appropriate. In all cases, your answers will be kept strictly confidential. (READ, IF NECESSARY: Because we have scientifically chosen the telephone numbers, your cooperation is especially important.)

A unique formatting challenge occurs when several household members need to be interviewed in the same survey. It would be cumbersome and wasteful to fill out a separate interview booklet on each household member. Instead, a format can be devised where the questions are on one side of the interview booklet and the answer columns on the facing side. Each answer column is labeled for the responses of one of the household members. Thus the responses of all household members are contained in one packet (see Example 2.20).

EXAMPLE 2.20
Multicolumn Format for Interviewing
Multiple Household Members

QUESTIONS (Page 1)	HOUSEHOLD MEMBERS (Page 2)			
	Respondent 1 (R1)	Respondent 2	Respondent 3	Respondent 4
	Birth Date __/__/__	Birth Date __/__/__	Birth Date __/__/__	Birth Date __/__/__
		Relationship to R1:	Relationship to R1:	Relationship to R1:
1. Have you ever smoked cigarettes?	Y.....1 N.....2	Y.....1 N.....2	Y.....1 N.....2	Y.....1 N.....2
2. Have you ever smoked cigars?	Y.....1 N.....2	Y.....1 N.....2	Y.....1 N.....2	Y.....1 N.....2

The birth date of each respondent in the household is listed as an identifier in the response column. All answers given by that respondent are recorded in the same column. A great deal of paper is saved using this strategy.

Question Order

Formatting questions and instructions is one challenge; the order of placement of questions is another. Whether it is to be administered by telephone or in person, the first items in the questionnaire must maintain respondent interest and make responding easy. The questions should usually be related to the topic of the interview as expressed in the introductory statement. This means that background or demographic factors, such as age, income, or marital status, are not the first questions. When the questions flow logically from the introduction respondents are drawn into the interview rather than being distracted and perhaps annoyed by questions they consider irrelevant (but which the surveyor may need answered at some point for statistical purposes). A smooth start also sets the tone for the rest of the interview, establishing a "rapport effect" that builds trust and enhances willingness to participate fully in the interview. The first questions should be easy to understand and nonthreatening.

Once respondents have been drawn into the interview, complex or difficult-to-answer questions may be introduced. These should be asked before respondent fatigue becomes an issue, as responses will be less careful and likely less accurate if respondents are weary of the process. Easy-to-answer items, such as demographics, should be placed at the end of the interview. Such questions are least likely to be affected by fatigue, and because they are personal in nature are best answered after significant rapport has been established. The order of questions intended to reconstruct a history, such as a job history, should be chronological, either forward or backward, to assist respondent recall.

When ordering questions for optimal flow, one must consider the possibility of **question order effects,** or situations in which responses to certain questions may consciously or unconsciously influence how a respondent answers later items. This is a significant source of response error. Although not always easy to anticipate or avoid, three such effects are common: consistency, fatigue, and redundancy.

CONSISTENCY EFFECT

This effect occurs when a respondent feels that responses to an item must be brought into consistency with responses to earlier items. This might occur, for example, if questions about the personal life and character of a presidential candidate precede questions about competence for office. The respondent might feel that judgment about competence should be consistent with the responses given on the character questions. This context might not be present had the competence questions been asked first. The respondent might then have focused on intellectual competence, for example. The effect can be far more subtle than in this example and should always be kept in mind when ordering questions.

Dispersing items so they are farther apart in the questionnaire probably does not reduce the consistency effect much. One must use intuition and logic in deciding which sets of questions might influence responses to others.

FATIGUE EFFECT

This effect occurs if the respondent begins to grow weary or bored over the course of the interview. At the beginning, much thought may be given to answering informatively, but later, the respondent may begin to give incomplete answers or choose to omit difficult questions. Fatigue can set in after several related questions. It is useful to use transitions and variations of question or response form to recapture the respondent's attention. It also helps to put easy-to-answer questions at the end.

REDUNDANCY EFFECT

Respondents may not answer a question carefully, if at all, when it seems to repeat a previous question. When items are similar but distinct in the mind of the surveyor, differences need to be clearly pointed out. For example, questions regarding smoking history may begin with something general, such as "Have you ever smoked cigarettes?" A later question, designed in the mind of the surveyor to distinguish current smokers from past smokers, may read "Do you smoke cigarettes?" A respondent may not recognize the difference in meaning just from the context, especially if the second question does not immediately follow the first. The questions might be more clearly worded this way: "Have you **ever** smoked cigarettes (any time in your life)?" and "Do you **currently** (in the past 6 months) smoke cigarettes?"

Response Order

An issue similar to question order is the effect of **response** order on answers chosen by respondents. Response order is of greater concern with telephone interviews than with in-person ones. The answer given by the respondent can have more to do with the order of the options than their content. It is again the inability to use visual aids with lists of printed response options that makes this more of a concern in the telephone interview.

There are three sources of response order bias:

- Memory errors—The respondent loses track of all of the options and picks one that comes to mind easily rather than the most accurate one.

- "Primary" or "recency" effect—The tendency of the respondent to choose the first or last response regardless of content; this occurs with long lists and with rating scales (e.g., agree/disagree).
- Respondents' tendency with lists followed by rating scales (e.g., excellent/fair; approve/disapprove) to acquiesce or agree with the items regardless of their true feelings.

The latter phenomenon is referred to as **response set,** or the tendency to reply to attitude scale questions in the same manner regardless of the content of the question. For example, in a matrix question where respondents are asked to indicate the extent to which they agree or disagree with a series of statements, they tend to answer all consistently (e.g., "agree") without considering the content of each item or treating each item as an independent question.

It is advisable, especially for telephone interviews, to limit the number of response categories to four or five and to read them as part of the question to maintain continuity and a conversational tone. Lists with rating scales should be kept short (six or seven items) to reduce the likelihood of response set. When visual aids are used, longer lists can be tolerated better because it is easier to probe to make sure the respondent considered all the categories.

Question Grouping

For smooth reading and easy comprehension, questions should be grouped by topic, allowing the respondent to recognize relationships among questions. For example, questions about smoking behaviors should be grouped together, and questions about health problems should be grouped separately.

Although other groupings might seem logical to the surveyor who has analysis purposes in mind (a smoking question followed by a question about a health problem thought to be related to smoking), such groupings might seem illogical and confusing to the respondent and could have effects on response accuracy. It is better to group questions according to topic and reorder them later for analysis purposes.

When moving from one group of questions to the next, flow is maintained by the use of **transition statements.** These alert the respondent that a topic change is occurring and that the next set of questions is not dependent on the previous set. A good transition statement identifies the change of context for the respondent by giving information about the next set of questions. This information can reflect a change in the following:

- *Response pattern* (e.g., "Okay, the next set of questions has different possible answers from the one we just finished. Please answer the next set of questions with a simple yes or no.")
- *Conceptual level* (e.g., "The previous questions asked about what you know about gun control laws. Now I'd like to ask some questions about your **feelings** toward these laws.")
- *Level of complexity* (e.g., "Now that we have discussed these general issues, I'd like to ask you some more detailed questions on some specific topics.")

The statement may simply tell the respondent what topic the interviewer is going to address next. These statements should be used freely throughout the questionnaire to give the respondent a sense of movement through the interview and to provide an overall coherence among its parts. Example 2.21 shows the use of transition statements throughout an interview. Note that the statements are capitalized to catch the interviewer's attention.

EXAMPLE 2.21
Set of Transition Statements
Used in an Interview

1. FIRST, I'D LIKE TO START BY ASKING YOU SOME GENERAL QUESTIONS ABOUT YOURSELF.

2. NOW I WOULD LIKE TO LEARN MORE ABOUT MEMBERS OF YOUR FAMILY.

3. NOW I AM GOING TO ASK YOU SOME QUESTIONS ABOUT THE NONPRESCRIPTION MEDICATIONS THAT YOU MAY HAVE USED DURING THE PAST YEAR.

4. NEXT I WOULD LIKE TO ASK YOU SOME QUESTIONS ABOUT YOUR RECENT LEVEL OF PHYSICAL ACTIVITY, AND THEN I WILL ASK YOU SOME QUESTIONS ABOUT YOUR ACTIVITY 10 YEARS AGO.

5. NOW I WOULD LIKE TO ASK YOU SOME QUESTIONS ABOUT HOW OFTEN YOU ARE EXPOSED TO THE SUN AND HOW SENSITIVE YOUR SKIN IS TO SUN EXPOSURE.

6. NOW I AM GOING TO ASK YOU SOME QUESTIONS ABOUT YOUR TYPICAL EATING HABITS IN THE PAST YEAR.

7. NOW I AM GOING TO ASK YOU SOME QUESTIONS ABOUT SMOKING.

8. NOW I WOULD LIKE TO ASK YOU A FEW QUESTIONS ABOUT YOUR CURRENT AND PAST WEIGHT. THESE QUESTIONS ARE AN IMPORTANT PART OF THIS STUDY, SO PLEASE TRY TO ANSWER AS ACCURATELY AS YOU CAN.

9. WE ARE ALMOST FINISHED WITH THE INTERVIEW. I JUST HAVE A FEW STATISTICAL QUESTIONS THAT ARE USED TO GROUP YOUR ANSWERS WITH THOSE OF OTHER PEOPLE WHO ARE BEING INTERVIEWED.

10. THIS COMPLETES OUR INTERVIEW. THANK YOU FOR TAKING THE TIME TO ANSWER THESE QUESTIONS. DO YOU HAVE ANY COMMENTS YOU WOULD LIKE TO ADD?

Summary Guidelines

The following guidelines summarize some of the points about questionnaire construction made throughout this chapter.

Formatting Questions

- The needs of the interviewer, respondent, and coder should be considered in formatting questions.

- Treat all questions as part of a whole, not isolated or separate from other items.

- Arrange items and instructions for maximum readability by the interviewer. Do not break questions between pages. Provide adequate spacing in the text. Ensure that the interviewer does not have to page back and forth during questionnaire administration.

- Use different typefaces, graphics, and spacing to clearly distinguish questions from response categories and from instructions.

- Vary response patterns and group topics as often as practical. Response set and fatigue can affect responses after six or more items of similar interest or form.

- Get input from interviewers and coders on questionnaire design.

- Precode questions whenever possible.

Ordering Questions

- Reflect the focus of the research in the first question, as stated in the introduction to the interview. Choose easy items to start.
- Place any complex, difficult, or sensitive questions after rapport has been established but before respondent fatigue might set in.
- Place easy-to-answer questions, such as demographics, at the end of the interview to minimize inadequate responses due to respondent fatigue.
- Order questions in a logical way that makes sense to the respondent.
- Consider question order effects when arranging items. For the same topic, order items from general to specific, unless respondents are expected to be unknowledgeable about the subject matter. Consider using funneling techniques.

Grouping Questions

- Group questions according to topic. Arrange the groupings in an order that makes sense to the respondent.
- Use transition statements freely.

Pretests

The final step in preparing a questionnaire is to pretest it to determine if the parts of the questionnaire do not flow well and if there are unclear questions that need to be rewritten. Once the instrument is refined and finalized, the rest of the job of quality data collection is up to the interviewer.

Not only should pretesting be conducted on members of the relevant population, the instrument should also be pretested on interviewers and coders. These individuals can provide valuable feedback on the mechanics of the administration of the interview schedule, particularly on the quality of question flow, the accuracy and adequacy of instructions, the procedure for recording responses, the quality of the introduction, and the wording of questions. These individuals have a good idea of which question order and format will work or not work by virtue of their experience.

Pretests also give the surveyor a chance to experiment with sampling procedures, particularly the technique that will be used to select a member of a household. Of course, pretests provide an excellent training opportunity for all personnel involved in the survey.

One caveat is necessary here: It is possible to pretest too much. That is, seeking advice from others can be counterproductive, particularly when these individuals want to add some questions on their favorite topic or provide a very, very detailed critique. Because designing survey questionnaires is somewhat of an art, the perfect questionnaire will never exist, and all the pretests and consulting in the world will not produce perfection. Pretests are necessary, but sometime the line must be drawn and the questionnaire put into the field.

3 Interviewer Selection and Training

A well-designed questionnaire alone does not ensure valid data gathering for an interview survey. Interviewers who possess the right combination of abilities, knowledge, and skills must administer the questionnaire for optimal results. Data quality can be compromised by biased questioning styles, improper clarification techniques, inaccurate recording of responses, asking questions out of sequence or skipping questions, or failing to establish proper rapport with the respondent. As stated earlier, poor interviewing can compromise the quality of the best-designed questionnaire. A good interviewer uses unbiased questioning techniques, proper clarifications, and correct question order and establishes rapport with the respondent. Good interviewing is the result of quality train-ing combined with an interviewer's natural abilities.

Roles

A skilled interviewer enhances the collection of reliable and valid data through artful application of standardized interview-ing procedures. Successful interviewers use these procedures to perform three major roles:

- Maximize the number of completed interviews by keeping refusals and early terminations of interviews to a minimum
- Motivate respondents to participate thoughtfully by deliver-ing the introductory statement, answering respondent ques-tions, and engaging the respondent in the interview process
- Administer the questionnaire by asking questions, recording answers, and probing incomplete responses

To perform these roles well, interviewers must possess a combination of specific abilities, knowledge, and skills.

ABILITIES

Abilities are those underlying capacities that an interviewer must have to perform the basic tasks of the job without special training. An interviewer must, for example, be able to read and comprehend the interview, record the responses, work during hours when respondents can be reached, and, in the case of in-person interviewing, get to the interview site.

Abilities required of interviewers are the following:

- Speak clearly and use correct grammar in the language of the interview

- Read in the language of the interview to deliver written statements and question sequences without pauses and to understand written instructions

- Write in the language of the interview to record verbatim responses accurately with proper spelling

- Recall responses long enough to record them accurately

- Perform several tasks simultaneously: read questions, record answers, and follow instructions

- Work flexible hours, usually including evenings and weekends

- Travel to the interview site if conducting interviews in person

- Access a telephone for interviewing, unless the survey project has a central calling unit

- Participate in one or more formal training sessions to acquire specific knowledge and skills required for performing interviews

- Judge nonverbal and verbal cues of respondent so as to know when to administer reinforcement and clarification

- Exercise self-discipline and regulate verbal and nonverbal behavior so as not to improperly influence responses

KNOWLEDGE

Knowledge is the body of facts and principles that interviewers must internalize to perform the interview well. The requisite knowledge can be taught during formal training sessions, but above all, interviewers must understand that the interviewing role is a neutral one: The interviewer's task is to obtain information that is as truthful and accurate as possible. In other words, the interviewer should not be a source of error or inaccuracy.

Knowledge required by interviewers encompasses the following:

- Role of the interviewer in conducting surveys
- Understanding why maintaining neutrality is important during an interview
- Information about the survey project sufficient to answer respondent questions
- Objectives of the survey
- Techniques of minimizing refusal rates
- Principle of confidentiality as the most important means of protecting the identity of the respondent and the integrity of the data-collection enterprise
- Procedures for contacting respondents and introducing the survey
- Correct procedures for asking questions
- Techniques of probing during an interview
- Procedures for recording answers
- Rules for handling interpersonal aspects of the interview
- Administrative procedures related to project operation, such as filling out call sheets, mileage logs, reimbursement forms, and time sheets

SKILLS

Skills are capabilities to do specific tasks well. These capabilities may arise from talent, practice, or training (usually a combination thereof). A skilled interviewer *does* the tasks of the job well. A note of caution: Persons with telemarketing experience do not always make the best interviewers. They may have the skill to get a respondent to commit to the interview, but they often move through the questionnaire at an uncomfortable pace, skip questions, and treat respondents in a less than respectful manner. These persons need the training sessions despite their experience.

Skills required of interviewers are the following:

- Initiate and maintain a conversation with a stranger
- Respond professionally to unexpected questions and situations
- Remain neutral by keeping personal opinions out of the interview process
- Motivate reluctant respondents to participate in the interview
- Deliver the questionnaire in a flowing, conversational manner
- Probe incomplete responses in an unbiased manner for more useful results

Selection Process

Interviewing is a difficult job. Selecting interviewers for a particular survey involves recruiting applicants, evaluating their qualifications for becoming good interviewers (reviewing resumés and conducting job interviews), and offering positions to the most qualified candidates. A small survey with few resources may choose from among existing staff at the organization conducting the survey; a larger operation may formally recruit candidates from outside. In either case, it is important to select interviewers with the most promising characteristics and abilities because, as stated previously, not everyone has the potential to be a good interviewer.

Interviewer characteristics, such as gender, race, or age, apparently have no consistent effects on response. Nor is experience a factor in producing differential response rates. The voice of the telephone interviewer would seem crucial, but little is known about the impact of voice quality except that interviewers with slightly louder tones and the ability to pronounce distinctly have better response rates. An interviewer's personal appearance is more of a factor in interviews conducted in person, but just how much of an effect personal characteristics have on response rate is not known. There is some support for the practice of recruiting interviewers with the same characteristics as those of the population to be surveyed.

One factor that does seem to affect response rate is the expectation that an interviewer has of obtaining a completed questionnaire or being able to get a response to a difficult question or question sequence. Also, the higher the workload, the lower the response rates. Thus, allocating the workload in a reasonable and fair manner among interviewers who are optimistic about the prospect of obtaining responses should result in higher rates of completion for both telephone and in-person interviews.

JOB DESCRIPTION

The first step in identifying potential interviewers is to develop a **job description.** It describes the tasks and duties that an interviewer must perform on a specific survey project and lists the abilities, knowledge, and skills required to execute those tasks and duties. How detailed the job description is varies with the survey project. In general, a good job description contains four key sections:

Summary statement: Brief description of the purpose of the survey and the role of the interviewer

Description of supervision provided: How performance will be monitored and evaluated and what level of independence is expected

Duties and tasks: List of the components of the work the interviewer will be assigned (e.g., calling or visiting respondents, administering questionnaires, filling out forms)

Abilities, knowledge, and skills: List of the qualifications in specific terms of what a good interviewer must know and be able to do; the job description must specify which of these are required at the outset and which can be trained after hire

A sample job description is shown in Example 3.1.

EXAMPLE 3.1
Sample Job Description

Summary Statement	The Epilepsy Foundation of America® requires interviewers to administer a telephone survey of client quality of life. The survey will be administered under the auspices of selected Epilepsy Foundation affiliates to evaluate the effectiveness of a new quality-of-life assessment methodology. Affiliates will use this methodology to determine their effectiveness in improving the quality of life of their client populations and to assess continuing client needs.
Supervision	Under general supervision of an outside survey development team, interviewers will obtain questionnaire responses from selected clients by telephone. The survey team will train interviewers, monitor and evaluate completed interviews for accuracy and completeness, and provide feedback as necessary.

Duties and Tasks	Interviewer duties and tasks will include calling selected clients by telephone to enlist their cooperation in the survey and administering a structured questionnaire over the telephone, recording responses, and editing completed questionnaires for errors before submission to the survey team.
Abilities, Knowledge, and Skills	Interviewers must have good reading, writing, and speaking abilities to read questionnaire items according to skip patterns and record responses in English. They must also be available to conduct interviews during evening and weekend hours and to attend two half-day training sessions. Skills for maintaining confidentiality, administering questionnaires, and enlisting client cooperation will be trained.

The job description tells prospective interviewers what to expect of the job and what is expected of them if hired. It is used to advertise the availability of positions and recruit applicants. The required abilities, knowledge, and skills are matched to those listed on resumés in the process of screening applicants for job interviews. These qualifications are also used to formulate interview questions about an applicant's suitability for the job. Even if interviewers are being chosen from existing staff at an organization implementing its own survey, candidates should be screened and interviewed.

The best interviewers are those who have a certain intuition or talent for dealing with people in an engaging but professional manner. Intuition and talent are not measurable qualities. They will surface as trained interviewers begin testing their skills in practice sessions and on the job. Talented interviewers will likely stay on the job, whereas those lacking intuition will likely find the job unrewarding and drop out, although occasionally they may need to be removed from the job or reassigned to other tasks.

Training

Once interviewers have been selected and have accepted job offers, they must be trained. The depth and detail of the training materials will vary with the survey project. Training procedures will usually contain some combination of the following:

- Training Manual

  The training manual is an important document both for teaching interviewers how to do their jobs and as a reference on the job. The manual provides context for the interviewer, describes the interviewer's obligations, and outlines interviewing techniques. The next section of this chapter is devoted to a detailed discussion of the contents of the training manual.

- Lectures, Presentations, and Discussions

  Whenever possible, training procedures should include formal training sessions. During such sessions, the material in the training manual is presented orally by a trainer experienced in survey work and interviewing. Important skills and a model interview are demonstrated. A later section of this chapter focuses on the purpose and content of the training session.

- Practice

  The training sessions should provide trainees with ample opportunities for supervised practice. After seeing an interview demonstrated, trainees take turns role-playing the parts of both the interviewer and the respondent. Trainees also interview the trainer, who can ad lib difficult or unusual responses. The trainer observes the role-playing and gives direct feedback to trainees. If available, volunteer respondents (e.g., other survey staff members) may be brought in for trainees to interview after practicing among themselves. Trainees should be encouraged to perform as many simulated interviews (on friends, relatives, neighbors) as they can to become familiar with the interview. If the survey will be done by telephone, each trainee may be given an assignment to call the trainer on the telephone during the next week or two to conduct a mock interview. This gives the trainee the opportunity to get a sense of interviewing without eye contact and helps the trainer assess how the trainee comes across on the telephone. A mock in-person interview can also be set up for training and/or testing purposes.

■ Observation

If a new group of interviewers is being trained for an ongoing project, observation of veteran interviewers on the job can be useful for training. Listening in on telephone interviews is easily accomplished. Accompanying an interviewer on an in-person interview is also possible with the respondent's permission; however, survey administrators must weigh the possibility that the trainee's presence will influence the respondent's answers against the long-term advantages of well-trained interviewers. An alternative approach might be to have trainees listen to tape recordings of interviews.

Training Manual

Although many of the instructions given to interviewers are very similar from survey to survey, details and context will vary. Most surveys will require the development of a project-specific training manual. General topics to cover in a training manual are outlined in the following sample Table of Contents (Example 3.2). Each topic is then discussed briefly.

EXAMPLE 3.2
Sample Table of Contents of
an Interviewer Training Manual

Description of the Survey
Introduction to Survey Methods
Interviewing Techniques and Guidelines
    Preparing for the Interview
    Beginning the Interview
    Asking the Questions
    Probing
    Ending the Interview
The Interviewer's Responsibilities
    Contacting Respondents
    Confidentiality
    How to Use the Interview
    Editing the Interview
Item-by-Item Rationale for Interview Questions
Sample Interview
Forms and Administrative Procedures
    Interview Summary Form
    Control Sheet
    Call Record
    Time Sheets

SOURCE: Adapted from Kaiser/UCLA Sigmoid Study.

Description of the Survey: This section introduces the interviewer to the purpose of the survey in some detail, imparting the greater context within which interviews will be conducted. A description of the target population, sampling procedures used, and objectives of the survey is given. Key individuals, such as survey coordinators and collaborators, are named.

Introduction to Survey Methods: In this section, the basic steps of conducting surveys are outlined, emphasizing the interviewer's place in the process. The steps include data collection, coding, data entry, analysis, and reporting of results. The interviewer plays the key role in data collection and coding. The flow of data through the survey office, from interviewing through computer entry, and the nature of supervision to be provided for the project as a whole are described.

Interviewing Techniques and Guidelines: Statements about the following topics give the interviewer important information about how to conduct interviews.

Preparing for the Interview: Review of any materials and procedures the interviewer may still need practice with should precede the first phone call or field visit. Supplemental materials, such as introductory and fallback statements and visual aids, must be organized in advance for easy access.

Beginning the Interview: The initial stage of the interview conversation is about gaining cooperation. The interviewer and respondent need to establish good rapport at this stage. Cooperation can be gained by convincing the respondent that the survey is important and worthwhile. State the importance of a professional and friendly manner, well-delivered introductory statements, and successful answers to questions for engaging the respondent.

A discussion of the importance of the interviewer's own state of mind is appropriate here. The interviewer's personal conviction that the survey is worthwhile can help motivate respondents to participate. Tell the interviewer that success in engaging respondent interest at this point will minimize refusals, thus improving the chances of collecting unbiased data because more of the people initially chosen to participate contribute their views. Give interviewers suggested responses for dealing with refusal attempts (see Example 3.3).

EXAMPLE 3.3
Possible Responses to Refusal Attempts

Too busy · This should only take a few minutes. Sorry to have caught you at a bad time. I would be happy to call back. When would be a good time to call in the next day or two?

Bad health · I'm sorry to hear that. I would be happy to call back in a day or two. Would that be okay?

Too old · Older person's opinions are just as important in this survey as anyone else's. For the results to be representative, we have to be sure that older people have as much chance to give their opinion as anyone else does. We really want **your** opinion.

Feel inadequate · The questions are not at all difficult. There are no right or wrong answers. We are concerned about how you feel rather than how much you know about certain things. Some of the people we have already interviewed had the same concern you have, but once we got started they didn't have any difficulty answering the questions. Maybe I could read just a few questions to you so you can see what they are like.

Not interested	It's very important that we get the opinions of everyone in the sample. Otherwise, the results won't be very useful. So, I'd really like to talk with you.
No one's business	I can certainly understand. That's why all of our interviews are confidential. Protecting people's privacy is one of our major concerns, so we do not put people's names on the interview forms. All the results are reported in such a way that no individual can be linked with any answer.
Objects to surveys	The questions in this survey are ones that _(client)_ really needs answers to, and we think your opinions are important.
Objects to phone	We are doing this survey by telephone because we can reach a lot more people for a lot less cost.

Asking the Questions: Explain the importance of maintaining a neutral attitude when conducting interviews. A neutral manner is one that does not imply criticism, surprise, approval, or disapproval of anything the respondent says, or of anything contained in the questionnaire. The point is to refrain from any behaviors that could influence how the respondent answers the questions. Emphasize the need to ask all questions in the order presented and exactly as worded. The purpose of this is **standardization;** the less variation there is in the way interview questions are delivered from one interview to another and from one interviewer to another, the better the chances that answers will be comparable. Each respondent needs to **hear the same question** to ensure comparability of answers.

Tell the interviewer not to read response categories unless they are part of the question or the questionnaire instructs the interviewer to read them. During questionnaire preparation, thought was given to whether or not response options should be offered the respondent, depending on the nature of the question. It is the interviewer's job to make sure that the decisions made in question preparation are carried out to maximize data quality.

Explain the use of prompts if they are included in the questionnaire. Prompts are predetermined statements to be used when respondents seem confused or unclear about how to answer a question. For example, when asked how many cigarettes are smoked in a day, a hesitant respondent might be prompted with "A pack contains 20 cigarettes." Prompts are printed on the questionnaire near the item they support. They are read verbatim.

Probing: Probing is used to obtain more information if a respondent's answer is unclear, irrelevant, or incomplete. Probes may or may not be verbal. Remind the interviewer of the importance of keeping probes neutral, and give some examples (see Example 3.4).

EXAMPLE 3.4
Interview Probes

Show Interest. An expression of interest and understanding, such as "uh-huh," "I see," and "yes," conveys the message that the response has been heard and more is expected.

Pause. Silence can tell a respondent that you are waiting to hear more.

Repeat the Question. This can help a respondent who has not understood, misinterpreted, or strayed from the question to get back on track.

Repeat the Reply. This can stimulate the respondent to say more, or recognize an inaccuracy.

Ask a Neutral Question.

For Clarification:	"What do you mean exactly?"
	"Could you please explain that?"
For Specificity:	"Could you be more specific about that?"
	"Tell me about that. What, who, how, why?"
For Relevance:	"I see. Well, let me ask you again" (REPEAT QUESTION AS WRITTEN).
	"Would you tell me how you mean that?"
For Completeness:	"What else?"
	"Can you think of an example?"

SOURCE: Adapted from the Kaiser/UCLA Sigmiod Study.

Poor probes are those that make interpretations, as illustrated in Example 3.5.

EXAMPLE 3.5
Improper Probing

Question: "About how many hours of television would you say you watch in a 24-hour period?"

Answer: "Oh, I watch TV all day."

Improper Probe: "So you mean about 12 hours?"

Better Probe: "Could you be more specific? About how many **hours** would you say you watch in a 24-hour period?"

The improper probe puts words in the respondent's mouth. It is better to politely request a more specific answer without making any assumptions.

Ending the Interview: Let interviewers know the importance of thanking respondents and reinforcing the important role they have played by participating in the interview. Some time may be spent at this point answering questions the respondents may have and discussing concerns that may have come up regarding the content of the survey. In fact, depending on the content of the questionnaire, a short "debriefing" conversation may be a positive way to end the interview. The interview questions may have raised some emotional concerns for the respondent. For example, parents who have been questioned about their children's exposure to potentially toxic substances may have become fearful that their children are at risk for serious health problems. They may need to be reassured that no causative links between studied exposures and specific diseases are yet known to exist and that none may be found. A source of any information on what *is* known could be given at this time, if appropriate.

The Interviewer's Responsibilities: Tell the interviewer what he or she is expected to know and do.

Contacting Respondents: Give detailed instructions for how respondents are to be contacted. If this is done by telephone, describe when interviewers should make calls (days of the week and time of day), how interviewers will know what telephone numbers to call, and what to do in the case of no answers, busy signals, answering machines, wrong numbers, and unavailable respondents. Instructions might read as shown in Example 3.6.

EXAMPLE 3.6
Instructions for Contacting Respondents

Place calls to each telephone number listed on call sheets until you either reach a respondent or determine that the respondent cannot be reached at this number. Call at different times of the day and on different days of the week. The most productive times to call are weekday evenings after dinner and weekends, except Sunday morning. Time your last call so that it will end by 9 p.m., unless a respondent has asked you to call back late. If you get a busy signal or no answer, call back in 10 to 30 minutes. If you get an answering machine, leave a brief message about why you are calling and state that you will call back at another time. If you get a wrong number, verify that you dialed correctly. If a respondent is unavailable, politely ask when you might call back to catch the person at home. If someone agrees to an interview at a particular time, call back at that time.

If interviews will be done in person, tell the interviewer whether interviews will be conducted "cold" in the field after choosing a household according to a sampling procedure or will be scheduled in advance. If there is a sampling procedure, describe it. Make sure interviewers understand it well enough to implement it in the field. If advance contact is to be made, tell the interviewer how to go about it. For example, appointments may need to be made by telephone. Calls may need to be made at certain times of the day, as mentioned in Example 3.6. In-person interviewers also need to know what to do if no one is at home when they knock on a door—for example, how many times to return to the same household and whether to call to reschedule an appointment. "Stopping by" on the weekend to catch a respondent who previously agreed to an interview and then failed to be home at the appointed time is another option.

Be sure that interviewers understand internal procedures for tracking contact attempts. Tell interviewers how to identify interviews (usually using a numbering system) and how to record the outcome status of each interview. Forms should be prepared for this purpose and should include the time and date of the interview, its length, any problems encountered, and questions that a supervisor might need to answer. The interviewer can give an interpretation of the respondent's attitude toward surveys and reasons why a refusal or termination partway through the interview took place. This information is completed on a separate form but matched to the interview identification number. It is signed by the interviewer, and this document becomes the basis for determining the interviewer's productivity, or the number of completed interviews compared to hours worked. A sample of the summary form that interviewers complete is shown in Example 3.7.

EXAMPLE 3.7
Interview Summary Form

INTERVIEWER: Answer the following questions about the interview.

Interviewer _____ Date _____

Interview Start Time _____ End Time _____ Overtime _____

Which of the following best describes the respondent's attitude:

Very antagonistic 1
Somewhat antagonistic 2
Neutral 3
Somewhat helpful 4
Very helpful 5

How would you describe the respondent's interest in the interview?

Very *uninterested* 1

Somewhat *uninterested* 2

Neutral 3

Somewhat interested 4

Very interested 5

Did the respondent ask any questions about the survey?

Yes 1

No 2

Specify: _____

_____

ANSWER THE FOLLOWING *ONLY* IF THIS WAS A REFUSAL OR PARTIAL COMPLETION.

When did the respondent end the interview?
(Specify exact place—i.e., question number)

WHERE TERMINATED _____

Which best describes how the interview was terminated?

No warning or explanation 1

An explanation to which you were not given a
chance to respond 2

An explanation to which you *were* able to respond . 3

Please explain the exact situation under which the interview was terminated:

_____

_____

_____

Interviewer: _____
                        (signature)

Received and edited by: _____

Validation: _____

This form, along with the completed interview schedule, is turned in to someone at the survey center who will, in turn, edit the questionnaire for completeness, clarity in the recording of responses, and the status information. It may be necessary to have the original interviewer recontact the respondent to obtain responses to items that were either overlooked or answered unclearly.

Confidentiality: Devote a section of your training manual to the ethics of survey interviewing. It is extremely important that interviewers understand their ethical responsibility to maintain the confidentiality of the people interviewed. This means not only following protocol regarding not putting names on individual questionnaires but also conducting interviews in private settings and not sharing a person's responses with anyone.

The statements of confidentiality prepared for the introductory remarks of the interview should be reviewed thoroughly, and any internal procedures, such as keeping completed questionnaires in a locked cabinet, should be reviewed. Any identifier information, such as a name, address, or telephone number, should be removed from the completed interview. This is easily accomplished if this information is recorded on a separate cover sheet. Completed interviews should be stored in a secure location for a period of time following the survey until data entry is completed and the data files gleaned of improper codes. The interviews can then be destroyed.

Confidentiality is also protected when interviewers are admonished not to discuss any of the results during or after completion of the survey. Interviewers' assessment of the results of the survey is not representative because they interviewed only a small segment of the sample. As discussed previously, it is rare that the surveyor is not in possession of identifying information on the respondent (e.g., address, name, telephone number), so anonymity can almost never be granted. Thus, it is more appropriate to state that confdentiality will be protected rather than anonymity.

In all surveys, especially in those funded by government sources, it is necessary to provide for the conditions of **informed consent**. Informed consent is an absolute "must" if the respondents are somehow "at risk" by participating in the research. This is ordinarily not a problem in surveys, but it could be if extremely sensitive information, such as participation in deviant acts, is questioned or there is a potential invasion of privacy involved. Government criteria for informed consent include "what a reasonable person would want to know" (Frey, 1989, p. 248). The required items are as follows:

- Fair explanation of the procedures to be followed and their purpose
- Description of the discomfort or risk that might be experienced
- Description of the benefits that might be expected
- Offer to answer any inquiries concerning the procedure or intent of the research
- Instruction that respondents are free to withdraw their consent and to discontinue participation at any time

In telephone surveys, signed informed consent is almost impossible to obtain unless the consent form can be mailed and returned prior to commencement of the survey or is sent to the respondent after completion of the interview. Neither is done routinely because the respondent's identity is clearly defined. Thus, a request like "May I proceed?" or "OK?" is used, assuming the respondent is mature enough to make an informed decision about participating. Obtaining a signed consent form is not a problem with in-person surveys because the interviewer can hand the respondent a form to sign before the interview begins.

How to Use the Interview: Outline what the conventions in the interview format mean. The interviewer will need repeated exposure to these conventions to become comfortable using them. A set of possible conventions is described in Example 3.8.

EXAMPLE 3.8
Interview Format Conventions

Instructions to the interviewer are in italics. Italicized portions should not be read to the respondent. Skip patterns are identified using arrows followed by the number of the question you should move to next. Prompts are printed in bold face. Read them exactly as printed if the respondent seems unclear about answering the question.

Tell the interviewer how to record information (see Example 3.9).

EXAMPLE 3.9
Instructions for
Recording Information
on the Questionnaire

Write clearly, neatly, and legibly. Write "DK" when the respondent does not know the answer to a question. If you used a probe to get more information on a question, write "probed" in the margin. To record answers to precoded questions, circle the number of the response given. Answers to open-ended questions must be written verbatim. Do not paraphrase.

Editing the Interview: Editing is proofreading the completed questionnaire to find and correct errors, clarify handwriting, and add clarifying notes. Tell interviewers that they are expected to edit every questionnaire before turning it in and that a supervisor or other reviewer will do a second edit. If errors or incomplete sections are found, the interviewer will be asked to make corrections and possibly call the respondent back to fill in missing data.

Tell the interviewer how to record the status of the questionnaire in the process from interview completion through data entry. Many times, questionnaires will have a *control sheet* attached or incorporated into the cover sheet of the questionnaire. When a task is completed, the date of completion is recorded on the control sheet, and the questionnaire is routed to the next step. Example 3.10 illustrates the layout of a control sheet.

EXAMPLE 3.10
Control Sheet

STATUS	DATE	SIGNATURE
Interview Complete	_____	_____
Edit Complete	_____	_____
Corrections Complete	_____	_____
Data Entry Complete	_____	→ FILE

Once the interview is complete, the interviewer dates and signs the first line. When a reviewer has finished editing the questionnaire, the second line is dated and signed, and the questionnaire is routed back to the interviewer for corrections and callbacks, if necessary. On completion of corrections, the interviewer signs again and routes the questionnaire to data entry. Once data are entered, the questionnaire may be filed.

NOTE: Not every training manual will cover all of the described topics. There will be variations of what should be included and in what order depending on the survey, the experience level of the interviewers being trained, and the trainer's preferences. The following are some excerpts from a sample telephone interviewer's manual (Example 3.11).

EXAMPLE 3.11
Sample Training Manual
for Telephone Interviewers

General Interviewing Techniques Guidelines

A. NEUTRAL ROLE OF THE INTERVIEWER

The interviewer is a neutral medium through which questions and answers are transmitted. Therefore:

(1) Avoid interjecting your own opinions.

(2) Avoid being "clever."

(3) Avoid any unnecessary or overly enthusiastic reinforcement, such as "DY-NO-MITE!!"

(4) Be an "active" listener but only give the minimum of reinforcement, such as "OK," "I see," . . . [and] "uh-huh."

(5) Never suggest an answer.

. . . .

C. GENERAL TASKS OF THE INTERVIEWER

(1) Communicate questions accurately.

(2) Maximize the respondent's ability and willingness to answer.

(3) Listen actively to determine what is relevant.

(4) Probe to increase the validity, clarity, and completeness of the response.

Instructions to Interviewers

D. HOW MUCH INFORMATION TO GIVE

(1) Read questions precisely as written.

(2) I repeat, read them precisely as written. It is extremely important that everyone be asked the same question in the same way. Even a difference in one word could drastically change the meaning and thus the response.

(3) Information that you can provide to the respondent is listed below. . . . Do not go beyond this information to interpret questions from the respondent. Key phrases you might use to answer questions are:

"This is all the information available to us."

"We would like you to answer the question in terms of the way it is stated. Could I read it again for you?"

"I'm sorry, I don't have that information."

"I will write on the questionnaire the qualifications to your answer you have just mentioned."

(4) If the respondent still requires more information, call on the operations supervisor for assistance.

. . . .

E.   WHOSE OPINION TO ACCEPT

Everything should be in terms of what the RESPONDENT thinks—not the respondent's kids, friends, boss, bartender, etc. Therefore, you might need to say:

"I see. Now, is that what you think?"

"It's your opinion that we really want."

ALSO, DON'T GIVE RESPONDENT YOUR OPINION.

F. RECORD EVERY CALL YOU MAKE, even though the number was not working, no answer was received, or the interview was not completed.

. . . .

K. DO NOT TAKE ANYTHING HOME WITH YOU. All questionnaires, code sheets, instruction sheets, etc. must be left in the survey center.

. . . .

L. AFTER YOU HAVE LEFT THE SURVEY CENTER

We are adamant about the following:

The only way we can be successful is to establish and maintain a reputation for confidentiality. Therefore, please:

(1) Do not tell anyone the names or locations of people you interviewed.

(2) Do not tell anyone the substance of an interview or part of an interview no matter how fascinating or interesting it was. We find it rather disturbing to hear from other faculty members or students details of an interview 2 weeks after a study is completed. Confidentiality is essential!

SOURCE: Excerpted from *Survey Research by Telephone* (pp. 222-227), by J. H. Frey, 1989, Newbury Park, CA: Sage. Copyright 1989 by Sage Publications, Inc. Adapted with permission.

What Not to Do as an Interviewer
(excerpts from a handout)

NEVER

Get involved in long explanations of the study

Try to explain sampling in detail

Deviate from the study introduction, sequence of questions, or question wording

Try to justify or defend what you are doing

Try to explain procedures or wording

Suggest an answer or agree or disgree with an answer

Interpret the meaning of a question

Try to ask questions from memory

Rush the respondent

Patronize respondents

Dominate the interview

Let another person answer for the intended respondent

Interview someone you know

Falsify interviews

Improvise

Add response categories

Turn in a questionnaire without checking it over to be sure every question has been asked and its answer recorded

Item-by-Item Rationale for Interview Questions: A written explanation of the purpose of each interview item is useful to have in a training manual. Understanding the rationale behind the inclusion of individual items helps the interviewer recognize whether a response actually answers the question or needs a probe (see Example 3.12).

EXAMPLE 3.12
Rationale for Specific Interview Questions

Question: What is your current marital status?

Explanation: We are interested in the respondent's current (meaning most recent) marital status. Those people who live with someone other than a spouse will be picked up in Question 5 (Do you live with other family members or with someone else?).

Question: Think about the walking you typically do each day. On average, how many miles do you walk each day? Count the distance you walk for exercise, to work, as part of your job, to the bus, to the store, and so on. Don't try to estimate the distance you walk while inside your home or office.

_____ miles OR _____ blocks

Prompt: **A mile is equal to 12 city blocks.**

Explanation: The intent of this question is to estimate any **active walking** the respondent may do during the course of a typical day. Do not ask the respondent to estimate incidental walking that may take place at home or at work, such as walking to the refrigerator to get water or moving from desk to filing cabinet.

SOURCE: Adapted from the Kaiser/UCLA Sigmoid Study.

Sample Interview: A copy of the actual interview question-naire is important to have in the training manual. The inter-viewer needs to study the "real thing" in its entirety before practice interview attempts are made. If the questionnaire is not yet finished, use the most recent draft.

Forms and Administrative Procedures: Samples of forms, such as the Interview Summary Form (Example 3.7) and the Interview Control Sheet (Example 3.8), should be included in the training manual so the interviewer can learn how to fill them out. An especially important form is the call or contact record on which contact attempts are logged. By keeping track of interview contacts and outcomes, the surveyor gets a good idea of the level of response. These records also inform the surveyor of refusals that may have to be converted and call-backs that will have to be scheduled. The call records are analyzed every day to determine the progress of the survey, the response rate (which is calculated at the end of each interview-ing day), the productivity of interviewers, and to note any other field problems that may arise.

In large surveys, someone should be assigned the specific task of monitoring the status of every interview and sample unit contact. This person would also be responsible for distrib-uting new sample units. The call record is very important to quality control in surveys. A field contact record serves essen-tially the same purpose as a call record. It gives an account of field contact attempts and numbers of completed face-to-face interviews. Example 3.13 shows how a call record and a field contact record might be designed.

EXAMPLE 3.13
Call Record and Field Contact Record

Call Record

CALL RECORD				
Telephone Number: _____			Questionnaire ID: _____	
Contact Attempt	**Date**	**Time of Call**	**Outcome Code**	**Interviewer**
1				
2				
3				
4				
5				
6				
NOTES				

OUTCOME CODES:

    CI = Completed Interview   BZ = Busy Signal
    RF = Refusal   AM = Answering Machine
    NA = No Answer   DS = Disconnected
    CB = Call Back   WN = Wrong Number

A form like this one is used to keep track of call attempts for a particular phone number in a telephone survey. Each time the number is called, the date, time, and outcome of the attempt is recorded. Codes are used for each possible outcome. For example, if the line is busy, "BZ" is recorded in the Outcome Code column.

Field Contact Record

Period From: To:

Interviewer:

Date	Neighborhood Code	Interview Start Time	Interview End Time	Outcome

CI = Completed Interview   RF = Refusal
NH = Not Home   CB = Come Back

Mileage:

Date: Miles:

1.
2.
3.
4.
5.

Interviewer Signature: Total Hours:
Supervisor Signature: Total Miles:

This form may be used to document contact attempts in the field and how they turned out (e.g., respondent not home vs. interview completed) and the amount of time each interview took. In this example, the surveyor has chosen to include a mileage record on the same form for travel reimbursement purposes.

Other forms may also be used by survey interviewers, such as time sheets on which only the hours worked are recorded, and reimbursement forms for telephone bills (if calls are made from home) and any out-of-pocket expenses.

Training Session

Although some surveys may not require more than one day of training, in general, interviewers are much better prepared if they have had 2 to 5 days of instruction and practice. A sample training agenda is shown in Example 3.14.

EXAMPLE 3.14
Agenda for Interviewer Training Sessions

DAY 1

10:00 – 10:30	Introductions
	Review of the Training Manual: 1. Description of the Survey
10:30 – 11:30	2. Introduction to Survey Methods 3. Interviewing Techniques and Guidelines
11:30 – 12:30	4. The Interviewer's Responsibilities 5. Item-by-Item Rationale for Interview Questions

12:30 – 1:30	LUNCH
1:30 – 2:00	Interview Demonstration
2:00 – 4:00	Practice Interviewing (Role-Playing) Sample Interview Training Agenda
	DAY 2
10:00 – 11:00	Review of Interviewer's Responsibilities and Interviewing Techniques
11:00 – 12:30	Forms and Administrative Procedures
12:30 – 1:30	LUNCH
1:30 – 3:30	Practice Interviewing (Volunteer Respondents)
3:30 – 4:00	Wrap-Up and Practice Assignments

Training usually begins with a review of the training manual through presentation and discussion. The most important part of training, however, centers on interviewing techniques, which are demonstrated by skilled presenters who also give expert feedback to trainees during role-playing. It cannot be emphasized enough that repeated practice in both the training session(s) and as "home work" is essential for acquiring excellent interviewing skills.

Supervision

Training alone does not ensure maintenance of high-quality interviewing. Some mechanism of monitoring interviewer performance must be put in place. The importance of supervision has been mentioned many times in this book. There are four aspects of interviewer performance that require supervision:

- Cost
- Response Rate
- Quality of Completed Questionnaires
- Quality of Interviewing

COST

Interviewers can be "expensive" if the number of completed interviews for the time spent on the phone or in the field is low. This could be due to working at unproductive times, high refusal rates (a refusal can take as much time as an interview), or undisciplined work habits (i.e., finding other things to do). In the case of field interviewing, high mileage costs may be a problem if the interviewer lives far from the neighborhoods of the respondents. Supervisors need to look for these problems and give interviewers feedback, such as more productive times to work and review of procedures for minimizing refusals. Paying interviewers by the completed interview rather than by the hour can increase productivity, but could compromise quality if interviewers rush to get more interviews done. Quality checks need to be done.

RESPONSE RATE

High refusal rates should be investigated. If interviewers are assigned different samples of respondents, higher refusal rates in one group than another may not be due to the interviewer; the group being contacted may be harder to enlist. However, some interviewers will have problems engaging respondents adequately to get their cooperation. Supervisors can retrain interviewers in delivering introductory remarks. Some interviewers may never get the hang of it, however, and may need to be taken off the project. Those interviewers who *are* good at gaining respondent cooperation may be assigned by the supervisor to attempt "refusal conversions." Respondents who refused a first interview attempt are called back and a second attempt is made to convince them to participate. If done well, response rates can be raised somewhat with this practice.

QUALITY OF COMPLETED QUESTIONNAIRES

Supervisors should look for legible recording, correct following of skip patterns, answers complete enough for coding, and evidence that interviewers are recording responses to open-ended questions verbatim rather than paraphrasing.

Another task of the supervisor is validating that completed surveys were actually the result of an interview, rather than being made up by the interviewer. Although we would like to believe this never happens, the supervisor must do **validation callbacks** to a sample (about 10%) of respondents to make sure they recall having been interviewed, and to ask about the interviewer's conduct (see Example 3.15). A small sample of repeat questions can also be asked to see if they match the responses recorded by the interviewer. Knowing that periodic validation will be done helps motivate interviewers to do a good job.

EXAMPLE 3.15
Validation Callback Sheet

RESPONDENT'S NAME: _____

DATE OF INTERVIEW: _____

INTERVIEWER: _____

1. Was the interviewer on time? Courteous?

2. Did he/she hand you a map of your neighborhood at the beginning of the interview?

3. How long have you lived in that neighborhood?

4. Did you feel you had enough time to answer the questions?

5. Do you have any questions or comments regarding the interview?

QUALITY OF INTERVIEWING

To determine how well the interviewer conducted the interview, the supervisor must directly observe interviews. "Quality" means that appropriate introductions were made, questions were asked exactly as written, and probing was done appropriately and without bias. Telephone interviews may be observed with a supervisor listening in. In large telephone surveys, the supervisor may have listening equipment available for listening to entire interviews. In smaller surveys, the supervisor may simply be present in the room to listen to the interviewer, or interviews may be tape-recorded. For field interviews, the supervisor may randomly accompany the interviewer on a visit or may tape-record the interview. In this way, the supervisor can give feedback to interviewers to keep quality and standardization high.

Exercises

1. A school-based teen pregnancy prevention program plans a needs assessment to guide program improvements by interviewing students. It will be complicated to get necessary approvals to interview adolescents under the age of 18, so this process must be started as soon as a protocol is decided upon. Money is tight, but time is not limited by any particular deadlines. In developing the questionnaire the survey team will aim for an administration time of 20 minutes to be verified in a pretest. Interviews could be done by telephone, using a list of students and their telephone numbers obtained from each school. Interviews could also be done in person at each of the three schools the program serves. Students would be randomly selected from classrooms or in the cafeteria and invited to a private office or empty classroom to be interviewed. These are the survey's objectives:

   - Describe the experiences of teenagers related to teen pregnancy, either from personal experience or from the experiences of peers.

   - Describe student attitudes toward teen pregnancy and its consequences.

147

- Determine which program features students find useful and what improvements they recommend.

List the issues that should be considered in deciding whether to interview by telephone or in person.

2. The Epilepsy Foundation is planning a survey to describe the characteristics of persons with epilepsy in the United States. One of the characteristics is the types of seizures that people experience. Seizure types have different names, and individuals who have epilepsy may not know the medical names for the types of seizures they are having. One of the types is a *complex partial seizure.* During such seizures, a person may have an involuntary behavior, such as lip smacking, picking at one's clothes, saying something over and over again, staring ahead blankly, or not responding when spoken to. During a complex partial seizure, a person will always lose awareness and always lose touch with the environment but will not stiffen and jerk or have a convulsion.

   If you wanted to reliably ask respondents with epilepsy by telephone interview whether they have experienced this type of seizure in the past 12 months, how would you write the question? What technique would you use? If you were writing the question for an in-person interview, how would you do it?

3. For the following scenarios, name the question order effect that is operating and state how this problem might be overcome.

   a. About 20 minutes into a telephone interview, the interviewer asks the respondent to listen to a detailed paragraph about the welfare laws currently in effect in his or her state. The respondent is then asked for an opinion on these laws and is read four possible responses. He/she answers: "Uh, the last one, I guess." When the interviewer offers to repeat the question, the respondent says, "It's the last one. Let's keep going."

b. At the beginning of an interview, a respondent is asked what she/he has heard regarding allegations that a well-known actor was involved in a hit-and-run accident that injured a child. She/he answers that the details of the child's injuries were heartbreaking and the actor should be arrested. The respondent is later asked whether she/he would go to see the actor's soon-to-be-released next film. The respondent hesitates and finally says, "Well, I guess not."

c. At the beginning of an interview, the respondent is asked how often he/she exercises for leisure during a typical month. A later question is part of a series of questions about behaviors specifically engaged in to improve health. The question is fifth in a series of seven and reads "How often do you exercise during a typical month?" The respondent is irritated and says, "Like I said before, about three times."

4. You are a survey coordinator conducting a survey on changing knowledge, attitudes, and behavior regarding cigarette smoking for the California State Tobacco Control Program. The survey takes about 40 minutes and will be done by telephone interview of a large sample of California residents chosen by random digit dialing. You will set up a small calling unit with ordinary telephone equipment in an empty office at Tobacco Control headquarters. You will provide three half-days of interviewer training. The interview will be administered in English and in Spanish. Write a job description to guide your selection process.

5. In response to the open-ended question "How do you think drunk drivers should be dealt with by the law?", a respondent rambles uncomfortably about an incident in which a relative was arrested for drunk driving. The interviewer senses the respondent's discomfort and says, "I understand completely. I once had to bail my own son out of jail for drunk driving. Tell me, without worrying about this incident, how you think the law should deal with drunk drivers in general?" What is wrong with

this probe? Suggest a better probe the interviewer could have used.

6. Indicate how you would respond if the person you intended to interview said one or more of the following when you requested an interview:

a. "I don't know. How did you get my name anyway?"

b. "I am too busy now, but you can talk to my neighbor, Mrs. Jones. She likes to talk to people."

c. "I'm sorry, but I never give my opinion to others. How I feel about things is my business."

d. "Come in. We are having a little gabfest, but you can ask your questions anyway. I am sure my friends will not mind, and they can help out if there is a question I cannot answer."

e. "I can't talk right now. Come back in 2 months when I have more time."

f. "I don't know anything about the topic. You can talk to my wife. She is familiar with it."

g. "I don't care about the topic. I want to tell you how I feel about another issue."

h. "There is no need for you to come to my house. Can't we do this interview over the phone?"

i. "I can't do this at my apartment. Let's meet at Joe's Tavern down the street."

j. "Just how did you get my name, and what happens to the results?"

7. Assume that the following nine questions are to be part of a general population survey. Identify the flaw(s) in each question and rewrite the question into what you think is the correct format.

(1) I am going to read a list of recreation activities. Please tell me if you have regularly participated in these activities within the past 5 years.

(2) Do you feel that the public bus system operates in a timely manner?

Strongly Agree   Agree   Disagree   Strongly Disagree

(3) Currently, the United States spends $50-$75 billion on people on welfare who don't want to work. Do you think the amount should be:

   a. Increased
   b. Kept the same
   c. Decreased somewhat
   d. Decreased significantly
   e. Decreased a great deal

(4) Do you favor or oppose the governor's stand on gaming taxes and the suggestions for raising property tax?

   a. Favor   b. Oppose

(5) The city wants to build a football stadium on the university campus that will attract a professional team, create jobs, and bring national attention to the city. Do you favor or oppose the construction of such a stadium?

   a. Favor   b. Oppose

(6) If a nuclear repository would be located in the next 5 years within 100 miles of your favorite vacation place, would you change your route even if it meant going 75-100 miles out of your way when going to that destination?

   1 = Yes   2 = No

(7) The federal government plans to locate a nuclear repository 100 miles from Reno, Nevada. Would you be for or against locating the repository in the state?

1 = Yes   2 = No

(8) The DOE and NRC are concerned with cleaning up the environment. Do you trust these agencies to do a good job?

> 1 = No trust
> 2 = Some trust
> 3 = A great deal of trust
> 4 = Don't know

(9) What is your yearly family income after taxes?

> 1 = Under $25,000
> 2 = Between $25,000 and $100,000
> 3 = More than $100,000

Answers

1. *Funding.* Although money to do the survey is tight, in this case it is difficult to predict which interview mode would be more expensive. In-person interviews would all be done at the schools and thus require a minimum of driving around. Because teenagers may spend a great deal of time engaged in social activities away from home or may tie up the phone lines with long conversations, they might prove to be difficult to reach by telephone. Repeated callback attempts and fruitless calling sessions may make the telephone interview more expensive.

   Time. Time is not restrictive, so it need not be considered very seriously, especially because it is difficult to predict which mode would take more time. For the same reasons that telephone interviewing might be more expensive, it could also be more time consuming.

   Target population. There is no "logistic" reason why teenagers could not be interviewed by telephone or in person. However, adolescents cannot be expected to have telephone privacy in their homes, and their time at school is usually highly structured, making absences noticeable. As a group they are at a highly self-conscious phase of development and are significantly influenced by peer pressure. All of these characteristics may have an effect on data quality, depending on interview mode.

   Survey objectives. Again, it is not logistically impossible to meet the survey objectives by either interview mode. However, because the objectives require asking sensitive questions about possible personal experiences with pregnancy, respondents' replies in a telephone interview may be less informative and thus affect data quality. In general, such questions are more likely to be answered honestly when teenagers are interviewed in person, especially if interviewers are very well trained and have excellent interpersonal skills.

Data quality. The response rate in this example is closely intertwined with confidentiality issues and the need to ask sensitive questions. Response rate may be compromised if interviews are done by telephone because of the lack of privacy; teenagers may refuse to participate rather than risk having a conversation about pregnancy overheard by their parents. If interviews are done at school, they may still refuse because they might be seen leaving class or being picked out in the lunchroom; however, the interviewer has more control over the environment in the in-person interview setting. This provides a somewhat better chance of ensuring privacy (a reluctant subject might be approached while sitting alone in the library, for example, or offered a private time slot after school). In either case, it is very difficult to ensure confidentiality in this survey.

Because adolescents are self-conscious and influenced by peer pressure, susceptibility to *interviewer effects* and *socially desirable responses* may be high. Teenagers as a group may be especially likely to try to please the interviewer or represent the views of their friends rather than their own. The age of the interviewer, even as estimated by voice quality over the phone, might influence responses and could be significant in the in-person interview. When interviewer effects and socially desirable responses are considered, the telephone interview has a slight advantage. If the in-person format is chosen, questions, prompts, and probes should be designed with these considerations in mind, and the effect of interviewer age should be estimated in a pretest.

2. One option for the telephone interview is to use the funnel technique, asking a general, open-ended question first, followed by a series of specific questions:

   1. For the seizures you have had in the past 12 months, what generally happens?

         ===================================

   1a. For the seizures you have had in the past 12 months, please answer yes or no to whether you had each of the following involuntary behaviors:

Lip smacking	Y	N
Picking at your clothes	Y	N
Saying something over and over	Y	N
Staring ahead	Y	N
Not responding to people talking to you	Y	N

   1b. During the past 12 months, have you had seizures in which you *both* lost awareness and lost touch with your environment but did *not* stiffen and jerk?

               Yes   No

During the in-person interview, a description of a complex partial seizure may be given to a respondent to read, followed by the question "Have you had any complex partial seizures in the past 12 months?"

VISUAL AID:

COMPLEX PARTIAL SEIZURE - DESCRIPTION

During a COMPLEX PARTIAL SEIZURE you may:

> smack your lips, OR
> pick at your clothes, OR
> say something over and over, OR
> stare ahead, OR
> not respond to people talking to you.

During a COMPLEX PARTIAL SEIZURE,

> you will ALWAYS LOSE AWARENESS and
> ALWAYS LOSE TOUCH WITH YOUR ENVIRONMENT,
> but you will NOT STIFFEN AND JERK ALL OVER or have
> a convulsion.

SOURCE: Adapted from *Quality of Life and Seizures after Epilepsy Survey: Executive Summary and Final Report to the Agency for Health Care Policy and Research*, 1993.

3a. This is the fatigue effect. The respondent is tired and no longer willing to give thought to a complex question. When possible, place complex questions early in the interview.

3b. This is the consistency effect. The respondent may be reluctant to admit an interest in seeing the movie after expressing disapproval of the actor. The problem might be solved by reversing the order of the questions.

3c. This is the redundancy effect. The respondent has not perceived the difference between exercise in the context of leisure activities versus exercise for the express purpose of promoting health. The difference should be pointed out in each question, and examples could be given to clarify the distinction. First question: "How often do you exercise for leisure, activities you do for fun like hiking, water skiing, or biking, during a typical month?"

Later question: "How often do you exercise to maintain your health, such as jogging, working out at a gym, or swimming laps?"

4. One suggested format is the following:

JOB DESCRIPTION

Summary Statement

The California State Tobacco Control Program is sponsoring a survey on changing knowledge, attitudes, and behaviors related to cigarette smoking. Interviewers are sought to administer a 40-minute telephone questionnaire to English- and Spanish-speaking California residents.

Supervision

The survey coordinator will provide ongoing observation of interviews conducted from a central calling unit at Tobacco Control headquarters. The coordinator will supervise all aspects of interviewing, including monitoring and evaluating completed interviews for accuracy and completeness.

Duties and Tasks

Interviewer duties include telephoning potential respondents using a randomly generated list of telephone numbers, introducing and administering the survey to eligible respondents, and recording responses and editing completed interviews for errors before submission to the survey coordinator for review.

Abilities, Knowledge, and Skills

Excellent reading, writing, and speaking abilities in English and/or Spanish are required. Bilingual interviewers are preferred. Availability to conduct interviews during evening and weekend hours and to attend three half-day training sessions is required. Skills needed for maintaining confidentiality, administering questionnaires in an unbiased manner, and encouraging respondent participation will be trained.

---

5. The interviewer's own values have been interjected ("It's OK because it happened to me too"), and so he/she has reframed the question by telling the respondent not to include this personal experience in formulating a response. A better prompt would be "Uh-huh. I'm unclear about what you mean. Let me repeat the question."

6. Suggested responses to respondents' concerns and queries are the following:

   6a. "Your name was drawn at random (describe process, such as RDD). We do not know anything else about you. Your responses will be treated confidentially."

   6b. "We need to get people from all walks of life, not just those who like to talk. We need your opinion."

   6c. "This is very important research. We need your opinion because it will be valuable for the larger study. The interviewer will keep your responses confidential. No one will know which views are yours."

   6d. "We only want *your* opinion, and it would be better if I could interview you without your friends present. Could I come back at a more convenient time?"

   6e. "Actually, 2 months is too late. The study will be completed before then. Could I make an appointment to come back for the interview within the next week?"

   6f. "I'm sure your wife is very knowledgeable, but we really need to talk to the persons selected for the sample. I need to get your opinion and no one else's. It doesn't matter how well informed you are as we don't expect you to know all there is to know about (topic)."

   6g. "I'm sorry, I need to get your views on (topic). Can I ask you some questions first, and then you can tell me your views on (other topic)?"

6h. "This interview needs to be done in your home because there are some things you will need to look at that can't be described over the phone."

6i. "I would prefer to conduct the interview somewhere, like your home, where there are fewer distractions. Besides, if we do the interview in your home, it will probably take less time."

6j. "Your name was selected randomly from (name the list used). The results will be used by city and county officials as they develop policy in the coming year."

7. You might find several things wrong with each question, so there will be more than one way to rephrase the question into an acceptable format. Some of the suggested corrections are as follows:

Question 1. The term "regularly" is imprecise. It could refer to once a year or twice a week. Five years is also too long a time period for a respondent to recall an activity. You need to specify the time frame, say, within the past year or 6 months, and ask the respondent to recall "on average" if a longer period of time is used or to state exact number of times if a specific, shorter time referent is used. Telescoping is a problem with this type of question.

"I am going to read a list of recreation activities. For each, please tell me how many times you have participated in that activity in the past 2 months. First, how often have you played golf?"

Question 2. This question assumes both knowledge and behavior by making the presumption that the respondent is familiar with the bus system and has ridden the system. The answer categories of "Agree-Disagree" do not match the manner in which the question was asked. "Do you feel" suggests a simple "Yes-No" response. A filter question to determine knowledge of the system and ridership experience is necessary before asking the question on timeliness.

"The city has been operating a public transit bus system for approximately 3 years. Have you ridden one of the city buses within the past 3 months?"

      1 = Yes (GO TO QUESTION #_____)
      2 = No (GO TO QUESTION # _____)

If YES, "To what extent do the public buses reach scheduled stops on time? Is it nearly all of the time, about half the time, or are they rarely on time?"

      1 = Nearly all of the time
      2 = Half of the time
      3 = Rarely on time
      8 = Don't know

Question 3. This is what is called a "loaded" question because it biases the response. The amount of money spent is inflammatory as is the term "welfare"; the phrase "do not want to work" is biasing and a false premise and suggests a research agenda; the answer categories are imbalanced in a manner that reinforces the bias of the researcher. The $50-$75 billion figure may not be accurate. It is also better to number the response categories rather than use letters of the alphabet.

"Currently, the United States supports a number of programs designed to support individuals and families in need. Do you think that the amount spent on these programs should be increased, remain the same, or be decreased?"

      1 = Increased
      2 = Remain the same
      3 = Decreased
      8 = Don't know

Question 4. This is what is called a double question or a "double barrel" question that is really two questions in one. It also assumes that the respondent has knowledge of the governor's proposals on gaming tax and property tax. A filter question or keyword summary question could be used to either determine the level of knowledge or inform the respondent before asking the question.

"The governor has proposed increasing the state's revenue by making changes in the tax on gaming operations. Are you familiar with this proposal?"

> 1 = Yes (GO TO QUESTION # _____)
> 2 = No (GO TO QUESTION # _____)

Question 5. This is a "loaded" question biasing the response to a position favoring the construction of the stadium. It is also a triple question in that it addresses issues of national attention, jobs, and securing a professional franchise. This is a topic on which many will not have an opinion so a "Don't Know" response is needed.

"The city is considering building a football stadium on the university campus in the near future. At this time, do you favor or oppose this project?"

> 1 = Favor
> 2 = Oppose
> 8 = Don't know

Question 6. This is a hypothetical question that asks the respondent to predict future behavior. It is also a wordy and confusing question. It is probably a question better not asked, although impact assessment studies often use such items.

"If a nuclear waste repository were located within 100 miles of your favorite vacation spot, what is the *likelihood* that you would change your travel route to avoid going near the site? Is it very likely, somewhat likely, or not likely at all that you would change routes?"

> 1 = Very likely
> 2 = Somewhat likely
> 3 = Not likely at all
> 8 = Don't know

Question 7. This question has many problems. First, the federal government plans to locate the site of the repository near Las Vegas, not Reno. The question assumes the respondent knows about these plans. The response categories of "Yes-No" do not match the response "Favor-Oppose" required by the question. Locating the repository next to a city is not the same question as locating it in the state.

"The federal government is investigating the possibility of locating a high-level nuclear waste repository within 100 miles of Las Vegas at Yucca Mountain. Have you heard of this possibility?"

> 1 = Yes (GO TO QUESTION # _____)
> 2 = No (GO TO QUESTION # _____)

Question 8. Do not use abbreviations or acronyms such as DOE or NRC because not everyone knows what they mean. It is also a double question, as trust could apply to either or both agencies. The answer categories do not match the response requirements of the question. The fact that the term "concern" is used is potentially biasing in favor of the DOE and NRC environmental activity. It would be better to ask two questions.

"The Department of Energy, or DOE, has as part of its mission to work on behalf of the environment. To what extent do you trust the DOE to properly work to protect the environment? Do you trust the DOE a great deal, to some extent, or not at all?"

1 = A great deal
2 = To some extent
3 = Not at all
8 = Don't know

Question 9. The income question is always a difficult one to ask. In this case, the answer categories are too broad to accurately reflect the actual distribution in the population. Respondents will have a better idea of their income if they are asked to estimate gross rather than net income.

"What is your yearly family income before taxes?"

1 = Less than $15,000
2 = $15,001 to $25,000
3 = $25,001 to $35,000
4 = $35,001 to $45,000
5 = $45,001 to $55,000
6 = More than $55,000
8 = Don't know
9 = Refuse to answer

Suggested Readings

Converse, J. M., & Presser, S. (1986). *Survey questions: Handcrafting the standardized questionnaire.* Beverly Hills, CA: Sage.

Brief but excellent discussion of question writing and administration.

Converse, J. M., & Sherman, H. (1974). *Conversations at random: Survey research as interviewers see it.* New York: John Wiley.

Classic account of how interviewers perceive the task of interviewing, especially how they overcome respondent resistance and how a standardized list of questions is administered in somewhat unstandardized contexts.

Dillman, D. A. (1978). *Mail and telephone surveys.* New York: John Wiley.

Considered the definitive statement on how to conduct mail and telephone surveys. The Total Design Method has generated a lineage of research on stimulating response and reducing all types of errors associated with survey research.

Fowler, F. J., & Mangione, T. W. (1990). *Standardized survey interviewing*. Newbury Park, CA: Sage.

This text discusses recruiting, training, and supervision of interviewers, techniques of asking questions, and strategies for establishing a working relationship with respondents. Major focus is on reducing errors that might be attributed to the interviewing process.

Frey, J. H. (1989). *Survey research by telephone* (2nd ed.). Newbury Park, CA: Sage.

A review of sampling, questionnaire construction, question writing, and interviewing associated with telephone interviews. Includes extensive chapter comparing telephone, mail, face-to-face, and intercept surveys on several dimensions, such as cost, response rates, and data quality.

Frey, J. H., & Fontana, A. (1991). The group interview in social research. *Social Science Journal, 28,* 175-187.

A review of the various formats for group interviews that have been used in research settings. Both casual, informal field situations and formal, controlled contexts are conducive to this type of interview.

Gorden, R. L. (1987). *Interviewing: Strategy, techniques, and tactics* (4th ed.). Homewood, IL: Dorsey.

Extensive discussion of the factors that influence the dynamics of face-to-face interviewing. Discusses the appropriate setting for interviews and how an interviewer must deal with verbal and nonverbal communication in the interview context.

Gorden, R. L. (1992). *Basic interviewing skills*. Itasca, IL: Peacock.

Excellent review of all stages of the interview from designing relevant questions to establishing a proper atmosphere for interviewing, listening to the respondent, probing responses, and properly recording information.

Groves, R. M., & Kahn, R. L. (1979). *Surveys by telephone: A national comparison with personal interviews.* New York: Academic Press.

One of the first studies to compare telephone and face-to-face interviews on a variety of dimensions, including sampling, response rates, item nonresponse, cost, and response error. The comparison of RDD sampling design with area probability designs is a very important contribution of this text.

Hyman, H., et al. (1955). *Interviewing in social research.* Chicago: University of Chicago Press.

Good review of interviewing principles. Particularly important discussion of the impact of interviewer expectations.

Lavrakas, P. J. (1993). *Telephone survey methods: Sampling, selection, and supervision.* Newbury Park, CA: Sage.

This text focuses on sampling for telephone interviews, but it also contains two useful chapters on structuring the interview and supervising those doing the interviewing.

Morgan, D. L. (Ed.). (1993). *Successful focus groups.* Newbury Park, CA: Sage.

This anthology includes contributions from leading authorities in the use of group interviewing, especially focus groups, in research. The advantages and disadvantages of this type of research are clearly delineated in this volume. There are several accounts of how the group interview can be used to augment survey implementation.

Oppenheim, A. N. (1992). *Questionnaire design, interviewing, and attitude measurement.* New York: St. Martin's.

Excellent discussion of the issues of survey design, with especially valuable chapters on pilot studies, attitude measurement, and the characteristics of standardized interviewing.

Rossi, P. H., Wright, J. D., & Anderson, A. B. (Eds.). (1983). *Handbook of survey research.* New York: Academic Press.

Comprehensive and detailed review of all aspects of survey design, including sampling theory, measurement issues, survey administration, computerization, and data analysis. Chapters by Bradburn on "Response Effects" and Sheatsley on "Questionnaire Construction and Item Writing" are excellent discussions.

Schuman, H., & Presser, S. (1981). *Questions and answers in attitude surveys: Experiments on question form, wording, and context.* New York: Academic Press.

The authors use more than 30 national surveys conducted over a 6-year period to experiment with the open versus closed format, wording strategies, question order effects, and response order variations.

About the Authors

JAMES H. FREY is Chair of the Department of Sociology and Director of the Center for Survey Research at the University of Nevada, Las Vegas. He is author of *An Organizational Analysis of University-Environment Relations* (1977), *Government and Sport: The Public Policy Issues* (1985), and *Survey Research by Telephone* (2nd ed., 1989) and of numerous articles on question order, group interviewing, and response rates. He has also published in the fields of the sociology of work, sport and leisure, and risk perception. He has been principal investigator on a number of telephone, mail, and intercept survey projects, including regional and national surveys of risk perception, community needs and issues, and leisure participation patterns. He is currently completing a textbook on the sociology of sport and conducting research on delinquency and the impact of gambling on communities.

SABINE MERTENS OISHI, who holds a MsPH degree in epidemiology from the University of California, Los Angeles, is an independent consultant to health projects and programs in the areas of survey development and grant proposal preparation and a senior researcher with Arlene Fink Associates, Pacific Palisades, California, where she is engaged in program evaluations of health and social services programs and health professional training programs. She has participated in a variety of research projects at UCLA and the RAND Corporation, been a health sciences specialist at the Veterans Administration Medical Center in Sepulveda, California, and managed a division of the Department of Medicine at UCLA. She designed and implemented in-person surveys in urban and rural Liberia, West Africa, with the Liberian Ministry of Health and Social Welfare, U.S. Peace Corps, and USAID.